TRUSTEES OF THE MUSEUM OF MODERN ART

John Hay Whitney, *Chairman of the Board;* Henry Allen Moe, *1st Vice-Chairman;* William A. M. Burden, *2nd Vice-Chairman;* Sam A. Lewisohn, *3rd Vice-Chairman;* Nelson A. Rockefeller, *President;* Philip L. Goodwin, *1st Vice-President,* Mrs. David M. Levy, *2nd Vice-President;* Ranald H. Macdonald, *Treasurer;* John E. Abbott, Alfred H. Barr, Jr., Mrs. Robert Woods Bliss, Stephen C. Clark, Rene d'Harnoncourt, Walt Disney, Mrs. Edsel B. Ford, A. Conger Goodyear, Mrs. Simon Guggenheim, Wallace K. Harrison, James W. Husted, Mrs. Albert D. Lasker, Henry R. Luce, William S. Paley, Mrs. E. B. Parkinson, Mrs. Charles S. Payson, David Rockefeller, Beardsley Ruml, James Thrall Soby, Edward M. M. Warburg, Monroe Wheeler.

HONORARY TRUSTEES

Frederic Clay Bartlett, Mrs. W. Murray Crane, Duncan Phillips, Paul J. Sachs, Mrs. John S. Sheppard.

TRUSTEES OF THE CLEVELAND MUSEUM OF ART

William G. Mather, *President;* Leonard C. Hanna, Jr., *Vice-President;* Edward B. Greene, *Vice-President;* Lewis B. Williams, *Vice-President;* John H. Hord, *Treasurer;* Mrs. Benjamin P. Bole, Harold T. Clark, Ralph M. Coe, Mrs. Albert S. Ingalls, Severance A. Milliken, Laurence H. Norton, G. Garretson Wade.

William Mathewson Milliken, *Director;* Henry Sayles Francis, *Curator of Paintings;* Louise H. Burchfield, *Assistant Curator of Paintings.*

Frontispiece: Guitar and Bottle of Marc, 1930. Oil on canvas, 51¼ x 29".
Private collection, New York

GEORGES BRAQUE

BY HENRY R. HOPE

THE MUSEUM OF MODERN ART · NEW YORK

IN COLLABORATION WITH
THE CLEVELAND MUSEUM OF ART

ND
553
B86H6

ACKNOWLEDGMENT

On behalf of the Trustees of the Museum of Modern Art and the Cleveland Museum of Art, I wish to extend grateful acknowledgment to the artist and to the following persons for their esteemed collaboration as well as to all the lenders listed on page 4:

Jacques Jaujard, *Director of Arts and Letters for the Ministry of Education of France*

Georges Salles, *Director General of the Museums of France*

Jean Cassou, *Chief Curator, Musée National d'Art Moderne, Paris*

Bernard Dorival, *Curator, Musée National d'Art Moderne, Paris*

His Excellency Henri Hoppenot, *French Ambassador to Switzerland*

Georges Braque

Douglas Cooper

Daniel Henry Kahnweiler

Aimé Maeght

and Max Huggler, Berne; Robert Giron, Brussels; Con. P. Curran, Dublin; Mr. Saladin, Le Havre; A. M. Hammacher, Otterloo, The Netherlands; Rolf de Maré, Stockholm; H. Hoag, Strasbourg; Lucas Lichtenhan, Mrs. Sacher-Hoffman and George Schmidt in Basel and Louis Carré, Mr. Clayeux, Pierre Gaut, Albert S. Henraux, Mr. Herbet, Maurice Jardot, Miss Mariette Lachaud, Raoul La Roche, Henri Laurens, Mrs. Louise Léiris, Miss Lucienne Léonce-Rosenberg, Pierre Loeb, P. Martin, Henri Matisse, Mr. and Mrs. Paul Nelson and Henri-Pierre Roché in Paris.

In this country our efforts were supported by Alfred H. Barr, Jr., Georges de Batz, Mrs. Walter Camp, Jr., Walter P. Chrysler, Jr., Edward H. Dwight, Cesar de Hauke, Sidney Janis, Martin Jennings, Fiske Kimball, Samuel Kootz, Mrs. Ruth Maitland, Henri Marceau, Pierre Matisse, Miss Margaret Miller, Mr. and Mrs. Joseph Pulitzer, Jr., Perry Rathbone, John Rewald, Daniel Catton Rich, Paul Rosenberg, Theodore Schempp, Germain Seligmann, James Thrall Soby, Frederick A. Sweet, Justin K. Thannhauser, Mrs. Burton Tremaine, Jr., Curt Valentin and Monroe Wheeler who all contributed greatly to the success of this exhibition.

HENRY R. HOPE

LENDERS TO THE EXHIBITION

Mr. and Mrs. Leigh B. Block, Chicago; Georges Braque, Paris; Walter P. Chrysler, Jr., Warrenton, Va.; Stephen C. Clark, New York; Mme Marie Cuttoli, Paris; Chester Dale, New York; Richard S. Davis, Wayzata, Minn.; Mme Jacques Doucet, Neuilly-sur-Seine, France; Miss Katherine S. Dreier, Milford, Conn.; Roger Dutilleul, Paris; Dr. E. Friedrich, Zurich; A. E. Gallatin, New York; Mr. and Mrs. Leo Glass, New York; Mr. and Mrs. Abner Goldstone, New York; Georges Grammont, Paris; Mr. and Mrs. Jacques Helft, Buenos Aires; Miss Marion G. Hendrie, Cincinnati; Dr. and Mrs. F. R. Hensel, Indianapolis; Mr. and Mrs. Henry R. Hope, Bloomington, Ind.; André Lefebvre, Paris; Wright Ludington, Santa Barbara, Calif.; David Mann, New York; Mr. and Mrs. Samuel A. Marx, Chicago; Amédée J. Ozenfant, New York; Jean Paulhan, Paris; Mr. and Mrs. Joseph Pulitzer, Jr., St. Louis; The Reader's Digest, Pleasantville, N. Y.; Dr. G. F. Reber and Frau Erna Reber, Chailly-sur-Lausanne, Vaud, Switzerland; James William Reid, New York; Paul Rosenberg, New York; Mr. and Mrs. John Rood, Minneapolis; Hermann Rupf, Berne, Switzerland; Mr. and Mrs. M. Lincoln Schuster, New York; Mr. and Mrs. Otto L. Spaeth, New York; Louis E. Stern, New York; Mrs. Burton Tremaine, Jr., The Miller Company, Meriden, Conn.; Baron Von der Heydt, Ascona, Switzerland; Mrs. Edna K. Warner, Fort Lauderdale, Fla.

Albright Art Gallery, Buffalo, N. Y.; The Art Institute of Chicago; Musée National d'Art Moderne, Paris; The Philadelphia Museum of Art; City Art Museum of St. Louis; The Phillips Gallery, Washington, D. C.

Georges de Batz & Company, New York; Buchholz Gallery, New York; Galerie Maeght, Paris; Galerie Pierre, Paris; Norton Gallery and School of Art, West Palm Beach, Fla.

Copyright, 1949. The Museum of Modern Art, New York. Printed in the U.S.A.

CONTENTS

Photographed by Fritz Henle

G Braque

PREFACE

by Jean Cassou
Chief Curator, Le Musée National d'Art Moderne, Paris

Georges Braque was born in Argenteuil in 1882 and passed his childhood in Le Havre where his father was a painting contractor. Let us not hesitate to speak again here of all he owes to the skies of Normandy which have schooled so many painters since the days of romanticism and impressionism. Inspired also by his father's craft, he learned how to paint false woodgrain and false marble. An artisan's son, he himself is an artisan still. This perhaps is the profoundest secret of the perfections of the French: artisanship as well as artistry. Ingres used to stop his pupils in the street where a house painter was at work and say to them: "See how this man takes on the end of his brush just as much paint as he needs; neither too much nor too little."

Braque made his debut with the *fauves*, though at the same time influenced by certain Neo-Impressionists. He painted at that time with short, straight brushstrokes or little squares, as may be seen in the L'Estaque landscape in the Musée National d'Art Moderne in Paris, whose forthright chromatic colors are harmonized in a marvelous silvery light. It was during this sojourn in L'Estaque, in the years before 1910, that another trend of his talent developed: Cézanneism, leading to cubism.

Cubism according to Braque, cubism according to Picasso: the two ran parallel in their development, sometimes overlapping or combining. Nevertheless, to distinguish between the two has been made a subject of dissertation by art critics, almost like a theme for schoolboys' term papers. Picasso's cubism is Spanish: one occasion among others which he has seized, and will continue to seize, for the affirmation of his imperious and inexhaustible, fantastic and provocative genius. Braque's cubism, on the other hand, is French: a manifestation of unified personality, a search for reason and for method, an expression of a natural and naturally exquisite taste. The collages of the former are a kind of paradox as to the fundamentals of the painter's art; those of the latter reveal only his fervent and modest love of the materials in question, his submissiveness to whatever they may inspire.

7

The first world war, from which Braque returned seriously wounded, put a stop to all this revolutionary effervescence. By that time cubism had established itself as a matter of fact. It had upset universal concepts of art; artists felt obliged to study it and understand it; it was a necessary premise, a point of departure for the intellect in its reasoning about art. But each of the great artists who originated it developed thereafter his own individuality. That of Braque soon revealed itself as most singular, and his art proceeded to become one of the most original and highly perfected of our time.

Braque's idiom derived from all these previous researches and inventions. He has constantly found new profundities in them, and made them serve his purpose in masterpiece after masterpiece. For example, those still lifes and interiors with a palette delightfully selective, beiges and browns and grays dominant, with deeper sonorities in the later canvases. Figure pictures also appeared, especially monumental female forms, or silhouettes of sinuous or broken outlines. In all this, what seduces us at first glance is the particularity of his coloring, exact and sober and of a ravishing delicacy, and his orderly composition tending, as in everything he does, infallibly, undeviatingly and, as it were, fatefully, to a certain noble and simple grandeur. This same sure instinct is to be observed in the minuteness and refinement of his handling of textures, now silky, now rough, always sensuously delectable. The word for it is one which the critic now hesitates to use: beauty. Braque's painting is beautiful painting.

The spirit of the good and knowledgeable artisan has led Braque into the practice of various techniques, such as lithography, sculpture, low-reliefs and those curious recent objects which appear to be of archaic or Cretan inspiration. Here we feel the restlessness of his intelligence, of which something may be said at this point. Though he is fundamentally a practitioner of painting, producing this or that strange work, he is none the less, in his creative process, a meditative and reasoning man—theoretical, speculative and experimental. What he meditates upon and reasons about is the nature of the creative process, and the proper functioning of the creator. He has no set principle or preconception, but a full consciousness of what he is doing. In this he is one of the most complete artists I know and one whose presence, conversation and friendliness have inspired in me the greatest admiration, enjoyment and gratitude.

Brilliant intellect, lucid spirit, Braque knows how mysterious creation is. In all his vision he seeks not only to penetrate this mystery, but to preserve it. We have in the intimate notebooks precious evidence of this perpetual meditation of his. In between maxim and maxim are his sketches, tumultuous or reduced to essentials, spontaneous notations or intense research, caprices of mind, caprices of hand; in them all one can trace from step to step, the reactions of his genius to this or that simple object. An object of everyday life, miraculous enough: vase, plant, table, coal-scuttle, a woman's profile, all-absorbing and obsessive, to be seized upon and deformed and reformed, destroyed indeed and resuscitated from its destruction in that no less real and valid shadow, the form we shall see in a painting.

I have spoken of the maxims Braque writes in these notebooks. He takes pleasure in this kind of writing, which is a very French habit, in the classic tradition. Maxims, also, are a means of getting to the heart of realities and reducing them to small scope. Here we have moral rather than physical realities. They are the same thing, all a part of life to a mind as lively as that of Braque, a complete artist, a man to whom nothing of mankind is foreign. One has to be objective about life as well, in its sequence of experiences and ordeals. When one has made a maxim of this greatest of objects, by contraction and simplification, transformation and calculation, then the creative act is indeed fulfilled, the impact absorbed, the obsession resolved. Such is the image and the equation. Masterwork has been substituted for phenomena, perfection for disorder and drama.

In his ever present intelligence Braque has accepted and endured all his limitations; within them his free will has played. Braque's work is all self-aware, self-knowing. It judges and measures itself, and finds in itself ever new reasons to manifest a higher beauty. This modesty with regard to creativity and its laws and secrets, this no less robust and sagacious attitude toward nature and human life, this constitutes Braque's supremacy and greatness.

Writing as a Frenchman, addressing myself to the American public which has lately been shown no less significant retrospective exhibitions of the work of Bonnard and Matisse, let me assure you that Braque, too, is one of our great men. He brings to you transatlantic friends a message from that France which we hope will be eternal. He has all those virtues which seem to us peculiar to our nation which we intend to perpetuate: that divine modesty whose fruitfulness I have tried to indicate, the love of labor and of work well done, the appetite for knowledge and understanding, the determination to see things clearly, and an inalterable sense of human dignity. Braque excels in all these characteristics and ideals. Therefore he has indefatigably persevered in his life work, like a simple workman and, at the same time, a great aristocrat.

Considering his work as a whole, in its elegance, its discretion, its faultless determination, satisfactory to intellect and sensibility alike, we may unhesitatingly classify him with great predecessors: Le Nain, Chardin, Manet. The purest and deepest aspects of the French spirit are reflected and made eloquent in his genius.

TRANSLATED BY MONROE WHEELER

9

CHRONOLOGY

1882　Born, Argenteuil-sur-Seine, May 13

1890　Moved to Le Havre

1893　Entered *Lycée*; evening classes: *Ecole des Beaux-Arts*, Le Havre

1899　Withdrew from *Lycée* and became apprentice house painter

1900　Moved to Paris and continued apprenticeship

1901　Military service

1902-04　Art student in Paris: Académie Humbert, *Ecole des Beaux-Arts*. Summers in Normandy. Rented first studio in Paris

1906　Exhibited at *Salon des Indépendants*. Summer at Antwerp with Othon Friesz, first *fauve* paintings. Autumn at L'Estaque

1907　Exhibited at *Salon des Indépendants*. Summer at La Ciotat. Autumn at L'Estaque; change in style

1908　Spring and summer at L'Estaque: Cézanneism. Rejected by jury of *Salon d'Automne;* one-man show at Kahnweiler Gallery

1909　Exhibited at *Salon des Indépendants*. Friendship with Picasso begins. Summer at La Roche-Guyon

1910　Analytical cubism. Summer at L'Estaque

1911　Spring: first painting with letters. Summer at Céret with Picasso

1912　Synthetic cubism. Summer with Picasso at Sorgues. First collage

1914-15　Joined Army. Wounded at Carency. Given two citations

1916　Convalescent

1917　1st of twelve summers at Sorgues. Began to paint again

1918　Post-war cubism

1919　Exhibition at Léonce Rosenberg's gallery, *L'Effort Moderne*

1920　Beginning of new style

1922　Invitational exhibition at *Salon d'Automne*

1924　First exhibition at Paul Rosenberg Gallery. Ballet designs

1929　Summer at Dieppe

1930　Built cottage at Varengeville

1931　Thin period and neo-classic style; engraved plasters

1933　Large exhibition at Basel in April. Publication of Einstein monograph and special number of *Cahiers d'Art*

1936　New style of figure painting

1937　*The Yellow Tablecloth* won 1st prize, Carnegie Exhibition, Pittsburgh

1939　Retrospective Shows: Chicago, Washington, San Francisco. *The Yellow Tablecloth* won 1st prize, Golden Gate Exhibition. Sculpture

1940　Fled to Limousin and Pyrenees. Returned to Paris in fall

1944　First return to Varengeville since war

1945　Made Officer of Legion of Honor. Shows: Brussels, Amsterdam

1946　Exhibition in London

1947　Completed *Cahier de Georges Braque*. Show: Galerie Maeght

1948　*Billiard Table*, 1946, won 1st prize at Biennial Exhibition, Venice

GEORGES BRAQUE

EARLY YEARS THROUGH FAUVISM

Georges Braque was born on May 13, 1882 in Argenteuil, a small village on the Seine near Paris, known in the history of painting for the river scenes of Claude Monet in the 1870's. His paternal grandfather, his father, Charles Braque, and his mother, Augustine Johanet, were all born in Argenteuil. There were three children in the family: Georges, and two daughters. They lived at 40 rue de l'Hôtel Dieu in the grandfather's house, which is still standing today.

Braque's grandfather had a house-painting business which he shared with his son Charles, who was then a young man just entering his trade. In their spare time father and son did outdoor sketches around Argenteuil. Charles Braque was successful enough as a Sunday painter to enter his work in the *Salon des Artistes Français* in Paris. Braque still has a small canvas his father painted in the early eighties, a view of bridge and boats along the Seine, silvery gray in tone, but handled with a finish and style unusual in amateur work and reminiscent of Corot's landscapes of the 1860's.

In this environment of house painters and amateur artists, Braque began to draw at an early age. He was too young to have heard about Monet, but he does remember his father's telling him that many artists and writers had come from Paris to live in Argenteuil, and he watched the building of a house for Monsieur Caillebotte, who he later learned was the great collector of Impressionist paintings. There is little else of significance that he remembers about these early years; his beginnings at school, his joy in outdoor life along the river, the occasional trips to Paris by train.

In 1890,[1] Charles Braque, having found that he needed a larger territory for the development of his painting business, moved his family to Le Havre where he rented a house at 33 rue Jules Lecesne (this house was destroyed during the bombardment of the city in 1944). At first young Georges was homesick for the familiar countryside of Argenteuil, but soon he began to enjoy the activity of the large seaport: the wide estuary of the Seine, the beaches on the channel, the sailing ships and yachts in the harbor and the

11

life in a busy city. As he grew older he was fascinated by the colorful scenes along the waterfront: the sailors, the foreign languages, the brothels and cafés.

At the *Lycée*, Braque was an indifferent scholar; most of the studies bored him and he found it difficult to pay attention. For this reason, perhaps, he kept a little apart from the other pupils. Outside of school it was the same. He liked to walk by himself or go for long rides on his bicycle. In the summer he went swimming at the Channel beach or rowing on the river. When he was old enough, his father bought him a small sailboat. He used to sail up close to the big ships at anchor, especially the old sailing vessels which were still very plentiful. Thriving on the outdoor life at Le Havre, he grew tall and robust and developed a natural ease and skill in sports. The experiences of these years left him with a love for the sea and the country which he has never forgotten, and later, when he matured as an artist, he found his deepest inspiration through intimate and solitary communion with nature.

ART STUDENT AT LE HAVRE

Not long after he entered the *Lycée*, Braque began attending a night class in drawing at the *Ecole des Beaux-Arts* of Le Havre. He rarely missed the classes, which met every evening from eight to ten, and he sometimes went on Sunday mornings too. The teacher was a local painter named Courchet, who had a group of about twenty-five students. They worked mostly in charcoal from plaster casts of antique sculpture. After a year or two of this conventional drawing, Braque was allowed to enter the life class and try his hand at drawing from the model. Courchet had little knowledge of art but he was moderate and easy-going in his teaching and did not force the class to follow severe rules. Nevertheless, even in art school, Braque preferred to work by himself and paid little attention either to the instruction or to the affairs of the other students. His drawing was undistinguished and he was never given a prize or other recognition.

Although he had managed to keep up with his class at the *Lycée*, he was sure he could never pass the difficult examination for the baccalaureate and finally, at the age of seventeen, he withdrew from school. This move, which would have created consternation in a bourgeois family, was received with calmness and understanding by Charles Braque who had been hoping that his son would take up house painting as a profession. Braque wanted to spend all his time studying drawing and the fine arts, but this offered a dubious future, at best, and with little persuasion he agreed to learn the family business. It was doubtless reassuring to Braque that his father could follow this trade and still find time to paint pictures acceptable to a *Salon* jury.

In 1899, Braque became apprenticed to a local house painter named Roney, who had formerly worked for his father. He continued to attend the evening class at the *Ecole des Beaux-Arts* where he was now in oil painting. On Sundays he did outdoor sketching of landscape subjects.[2] He also began figure painting at this time, and did a portrait of his cousin, Louise Johanet (below). The face is modeled broadly in chiaroscuro, according to the prevailing academic style; the rest of the figure is loosely brushed in with rather dark colors. It is said to have a likeness to the sitter who still owns the picture, but it cannot have given much promise of success.

The collection of paintings in the Museum of Le Havre included nothing by its native son, Claude Monet, but there were one or two landscapes by Eugène Boudin, Monet's teacher at Le Havre. Braque admired these, and he was especially fond of the Corot landscape in the Museum. He also remembers the posters of Toulouse-Lautrec and other Parisian artists on the local billboards. But if he knew anything about the Impressionists, whose style of painting he was soon to adopt, it was only what he read in *Gil Blas* or learned from discussion with other art students.

Braque's social life in Le Havre did not vary from the conventional pattern of a provincial city. From time to time his parents took him to the theatre. His musical education began with lessons on the flute from a teacher named Dufy, a brother of the painters, Raoul and Jean. If he had any youthful romances, they were of little importance.

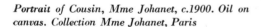

Portrait of Cousin, Mme Johanet, c.1900. Oil on canvas. Collection Mme Johanet, Paris

In the summer his family used to rent a cottage at Harfleur, a village on a small river near Le Havre. Braque enjoyed living in the country, and took many walks or bicycle rides in the region, often carrying his paint box along. His notion of painting followed the popular trend of the time towards subjects of the seaside or countryside sketched directly from nature. He seems to have picked up in a vague way the methods and techniques of the *plein air* school, and the pictures he did during the next three or four years were small impressionistic landscapes of mediocre quality.

The French law at that time required three years of military service, but this was reduced to one year for certain professions, among them that of a properly qualified artist. To obtain this qualification it was necessary to pass an examination and be certified by the *Ecole des Beaux-Arts*. Braque's un-cooperative attitude at the evening class gave him little chance to qualify. A similar reduction was granted to artist-craftsmen. There was some doubt as to whether the training he had begun with Roney would be acceptable to the draft authorities, and so at the end of the year 1900 he went to Paris where it was arranged for him to continue his apprenticeship with a painter-decorator named Laberthe who, like Roney, was a friend and former employee of his father's.

He rented a room on the rue des Trois Frères in Montmartre and enrolled in the evening art class of the *Cours Municipal* at Batignolles. This was directed by an elderly artist named Quignolot, who was friendly and en-couraging, allowing the students to draw as they wished. Occasionally on Sunday mornings Braque joined a group that painted at Quignolot's house.

He enjoyed his work as an apprentice. This was the second year and he now began to learn some of the special skills which were to appear much later in his pictures. Part of the stock in trade of French house painters was the ability to make imitations of the expensive materials found in houses of the wealthy bourgeois: gilt, polychrome marble, rare wood and masonry. Much of the interior decoration in houses of the middle class was done in this taste and the painter had to produce the effect of marble panels, hard-wood floors, and other costly surfaces by the skill of his brush. A good apprentice also had to know hand lettering and sign painting. In this way he acquired a knowledge of formulas and techniques, a skill in the handling of brushes and the application of paint; above all he learned the habits of patience and care which are fundamental in all good craftsmanship. These years of apprenticeship gave him a thorough technical knowledge which was to be a great asset in his development as an artist.

In October 1901, he started his year of military service. He was stationed near Le Havre and saw his family frequently. Among his friends in the bar-racks were Dieterle, the Paris art dealer, and Albert Henraux. Neither had any notion that Braque was an artist. They remember him as a big fellow who sang the regimental songs better than anyone else, rolled his own ciga-rettes and danced marvelously. After one year of military service, which he

View of Park at Honfleur, 1904. Oil on canvas. Collection the Musée du Havre

seems to have taken in his stride, obtaining the rank of non-commissioned officer, Braque was free to return to civilian life.

ART STUDENT IN PARIS

Braque's parents agreed that he should now devote all his time to art studies and they provided him with a modest allowance so that he could live in Paris. He rented a room on the rue Lepic in Montmartre and enrolled at the *Académie Humbert* on the Boulevard Rochechouart. Humbert was an academic painter and a member of the Institute. He could hardly be expected to have a sympathetic attitude toward the new trends in painting. Braque found, however, that he was allowed to paint as he chose, with relatively little criticism, as long as he paid his fees. While there he made the acquaintance of Picabia, who was then a fellow student, and also Marie Laurencin, who soon became one of his good friends.

After spending the summer with his parents at Harfleur, he decided to apply for admission to the *Ecole des Beaux-Arts* in Paris. Upon his return in the autumn, he went to see Léon Bonnat who was then the most famous

15

Ship in Harbor, Le Havre, c.1905. Oil on canvas. Private collection, Paris

teacher at the *Beaux-Arts*. Bonnat looked at some of his work and admitted the young art student to his atelier. Braque, however, was not happy in in this stronghold of academism. Bonnat's criticism and general attitude he found intolerable, and the students irritated him with their studio pranks. After a scant two months he left the Bonnat atelier and returned to the *Académie Humbert* with a feeling of relief. The experience left him with a pronounced dislike of academic art and teaching. It seems probable that thereafter Braque began to think of himself as a progressive artist and to associate with others who shared his tastes.

The summer of 1904 Braque stayed at Honfleur, the picturesque fisherman's village on the south shore of the Seine estuary that had long been a favorite with artists. Among those he met there were Raoul and Jean Dufy; one of Pissarro's sons, who remembers a sketch Braque gave to him; the sculptor Manolo; and the young art critic Maurice Raynal, who years later was to write a monograph on Braque.[3] A small painting he did that summer is now in the Museum of Le Havre. It is a view of the park at Honfleur, showing two figures seated in a public square, with the base of a monument at the left against a background of foliage. The details are brushed in broadly, the drawing uneven, the color rather dark. It has no particular distinction but is a routine example of his early efforts towards impressionism (page 15).

In the fall of 1904 Braque, having decided that there was nothing further to gain from art school, rented his own studio in Paris on the rue d'Orsel, opposite the *Théâtre Montmartre*. There he painted every day, sometimes hiring a model at seven francs an hour, sometimes working from still-life arrangements. In good weather he went out to do landscape sketches around Montmartre. He still considered his painting as student work and most of it he has since destroyed or lost.

During these first years in Paris, Braque studied the art of other periods, chiefly through his visits to the Louvre. What impressed him most, even at this date, was primitive art, especially Egyptian and archaic Greek sculpture. This preference for the primitives had long been developing among the younger artists.[4] Their bold, often crude designs were welcomed as a refreshing contrast from the familiar clichés of academic taste. (Picasso, when Derain showed him an African Negro sculpture, is said to have remarked "more beautiful than the *Venus de Milo*.") To the young artists of that group, the names of Phidias and Praxiteles, Raphael and Michelangelo stood for the institution across the river from the Louvre—the *Ecole des Beaux-Arts*, whose teachings and politics they cordially detested. Although Braque never cared much for the Renaissance masters, he admired Poussin. In Poussin's sense of order and restraint Braque found an expression of his own aspirations. But during these first years Corot was still his favorite painter.

At the same time Braque began to pay attention to contemporary art. He first saw the Impressionist pictures at Durand Ruel's and Vollard's in

Still Life with Jugs, 1906. Oil on canvas, 19¹¹⁄₁₆ x 24". Present owner unknown

Canal St. Martin, Paris, 1906. Oil on canvas, 19¹¹⁄₁₆ x 24″. Present owner unknown

the rue Laffitte. Renoir's *Moulin de la Galette* he especially admired. He was also fond of Monet, Sisley and Pissarro, but he never cared much for Degas. At Vollard's he did not at first notice the Cézannes, but he liked very much the two he saw in the Caillebotte Collection at the Luxembourg Museum. He has never liked Gauguin's painting, but he was much impressed by van Gogh, and also admired the paintings of Seurat and his Neo-Impressionist followers.

During the summer of 1905 Braque stayed for a while at Quimperlé in Brittany,[5] and also at Le Havre. One of his landscapes painted at Le Havre is a port scene, representing a sailing vessel tied up at the wharf (page 16). Composed with a large mass at one side, the design is sharper and cleaner than in his landscapes of the previous year at Honfleur. The colors are lighter and there seems to be a general improvement in quality.

THE FAUVE PERIOD

Late in 1905 the word *fauve* was adopted to describe painting in strong outlines and broad color planes, but the kind of painting to which the term was applied had been seen at certain exhibitions and galleries in Paris for

18

Port at Antwerp, 1906. Oil on canvas, 15 x 18⅛". Collection Baron Von der Heydt, Ascona, Switzerland

Landscape at L'Estaque, 1906. Oil on canvas, 28¾ x 23⅝". Collection Georges Grammont, Paris

two or three years. Matisse exhibited at the *Salon de la Nationale* until 1903 when he participated in the founding of the *Salon d'Automne*. The un-juried exhibitions of the *Salon des Indépendants* had also included paintings that might be termed *fauve*. At the Berthe Weill Gallery on the rue Victor Massé, many of the younger painters were invited to show their work; Matisse, Marquet, Dufy and Camoin exhibited there during the season of 1902-03, and not long after that Van Dongen, Derain and Vlaminck were welcomed to the group.

In 1905 Henri Matisse and the young André Derain, who had just been discharged from military service, went to Collioure where they painted a number of brilliantly colored landscapes that seem to have set an example for the others. Raoul Dufy, Albert Marquet and Othon Friesz painted landscapes along the Normandy coast that summer and although none was as bold as Derain, all three worked with bright color.

Friesz and Dufy came from Le Havre where Braque had known them for four or five years, and he was certainly familiar with their recent landscapes in bright color. But it was the still brighter color of the Collioure landscapes that impressed Braque the most. "Matisse and Derain opened the road for me," he recently remarked.

21

Seated Nude, 1906. Oil on canvas, 23½ x 19". Collection Mr. and Mrs. Jacques Helft, Buenos Aires

At the *Salon d'Automne* of 1905 the room assigned to this group made a sensation. In writing of these paintings the Paris art critic, Louis Vauxcelles, took advantage of an innocent statue in the center of the gallery, and made a pun about *Donatello parmi les fauves*. (In French this sounds like the expression for Daniel in the Lion's Den.) Soon everyone in Paris had heard of *"les fauves"* and their "cage" at the *Salon*. The principal artists represented in the room were Matisse, Rouault, Vlaminck, Manguin and Friesz.

The first public exhibition of Braque's works came in the spring of 1906 when he entered six paintings in the *Salon des Indépendants*. Since it was an un-juried exhibition, any artist had the right, upon payment of the twenty-five franc fee, to exhibit up to ten pictures. Braque sent several of the landscapes he had done at Le Havre during the previous summer and two still lifes. He recalls that the color in most of these was not so dark as in his earlier impressionistic paintings, but that it was not yet *fauve*. He must have begun to use bright colors in the spring of the year, during or just after the exhibition.

Braque and Othon Friesz spent the summer of 1906 in Antwerp, perhaps following the example of Matisse and Derain at Collioure. They found a cheap pension near the port and rented a studio on the banks of the Scheldt River with a balcony from which they had a view of the entire harbor.

For Braque this was a rare opportunity. At the age of twenty-four he had reached a new period in his artistic development. His style of painting was just beginning to emerge from conventional impressionistic sketches into compositions with more thought of design and color. Friesz, who was then twenty-seven, had been employing the bright colors of *fauvism* long enough to set Braque a convincing example. Both had grown up under impressionism and in their early work had attempted to paint the fleeting patterns of sunlight and shadow of the external world. To them the *fauve* style was hardly more than an extension of impressionism, with the added gaiety of substituting vivid pinks for pale lavenders.

Coming from Le Havre, whose harbor scenes both had known since childhood, they must have been delighted with the combination of the familiar and the foreign they found on the banks of the Scheldt. The marine subject matter lent itself particularly well to their aims in painting. The expanse of

Landscape at L'Estaque, 1907. Oil on canvas, 25⅝ x 31⅞". Present owner unknown

23

View from Hotel Mistral, 1907.
Oil on canvas, 31½ x 23⅝".
Present owner unknown

water and sky offered a natural composition of space and atmosphere and an easy pretext for introducing bright blues. Dufy and Marquet had already found a way of getting color and movement in their landscapes by introducing pennants fluttering at mastheads. The two young artists often used the same devices. In the new *fauve* style they painted many views of the harbor, the docks and the ships. At the end of the summer Braque had completed over a dozen canvases which he thought worth keeping.

The Antwerp landscapes, Braque considers his first creative work. They are handsomer and more original than his earlier paintings, but some reveal weaknesses that he had yet to overcome. Often his composition depended upon the device of a diagonal mass at the left side or along the base of the picture, which soon palls. Nor did he always achieve a harmonious balance between the treatment of deep space and the rather gay, informal surface patterns of *fauvism*. Nevertheless, the best of these Antwerp scenes have a charming decorative quality (page 19). They bear a strong resemblance, as might be expected, to the contemporaneous work of Friesz. One is also reminded of Dufy's landscapes of 1905-06 in the tonalities of dark blue, violet, rose and crimson.

Back in Paris in September he painted one or two views of the Canal Saint-Martin (page 18), but Braque was not interested in the traditional Parisian landscape subjects with their inevitable emphasis on the picturesque: bookstalls along the quais or the quaint streets of Montmartre. And now he no longer cared for the rare effects of light and atmosphere that had given inspiration to Monet. Braque needed an atmosphere of bright light and strong color. Considering his love for the sea it is not surprising that he decided to try the Mediterranean, where the climate was mild enough to make outdoor painting agreeable into the autumn and winter months. Braque selected the town of L'Estaque, on the coast just west of Marseilles where the foothills of the Alps make a magnificent crown around the bay— a view made famous in many Cézanne landscapes. He must have known that Cézanne had painted there but he thinks that other reasons caused his choice: the climate, the sea, the color, and the low cost of living. He paid

View of the Viaduct, 1907. Oil on canvas, 25⅝ x 31⅞". Present owner unknown

25

Large Nude, 1907. Oil on canvas, 55¾ x 40". Collection Mme Marie Cuttoli, Paris

about seventy francs a month for room and board at the Hotel Maurin where he stayed for several months painting views of the seaport, the hillsides, the houses and trees (page 21). Under the bright light of the Mediterranean sun, his color became a little paler, with emphasis upon pink and rose rather than the violet and crimson of the Antwerp pictures. He developed further the use of short brush strokes, applying pigment of medium thickness and occasionally dotting an area of water or sky with small squares like those of the Neo-Impressionists. The contours in his landscapes at L'Estaque are irregular and sketchy, but in some of them there is a better balance between surface pattern and spatial composition than in the Antwerp pictures.

Upon returning to Paris in the early spring, Braque decided to enter a group of these recent canvases in the *Salon des Indépendants*. He sent several landscapes, a figure painting and a still life. The figure painting, a seated, semi-draped nude in pink, lavender and green, resembles the *fauve* figures of Matisse in its treatment of perspective, its pattern and heavy outlines (page 22).

At the vernissage of this *Salon* in March, 1907, Braque made his public debut as a *fauve* artist. There he met Matisse, Derain, Vlaminck, Marquet, Van Dongen and others who were known as the *avant-garde* painters. To his delight all his pictures were sold; at prices of seventy-five to two hundred francs. One of the buyers was Wilhelm Uhde, the German collector who had "discovered" Henri Rousseau.

In May he returned to the south of France, this time going to La Ciotat, a small Mediterranean port and summer resort, a few miles east of Marseilles. Friesz joined him for the summer months and again they painted landscapes. Braque's paintings at La Ciotat are much the same in style as those he did at L'Estaque and unless one knows the two places it is difficult to tell the two series apart.

The distinctive quality in Braque's *fauve* landscapes is their warm pink tonality which is in marked contrast to the colors of Derain and Vlaminck. Indeed, there was perhaps a certain incompatibility between Braque and the *fauve* style. At any rate his interest in *fauvism* began to diminish before the year was over.

Braque left La Ciotat at the end of the summer, paid a second visit to L'Estaque and then returned to Paris. Some of the canvases done in the autumn of 1907 show an emphasis upon linear pattern quite different from his earlier *fauve* pictures. In one landscape of trees and mountains, the trunks and foliage are summarized in long curves which recall the *art nouveau* surface patterns of Gauguin and the synthetists (page 23). The change of style is also seen in a view from the Hotel Mistral at L'Estaque, showing three trees rising from behind a balustraded wall (page 24). The sweeping curves are now stiffened by many straight lines and there is a rigidity and angularity in the pattern which suggest the influence of

27

Cézanne. The color too had become paler, and he began to use a little green and brown, colors which had been taboo in his *fauve* landscapes. It is significant that this painting was done from memory after the artist had left L'Estaque. This is the first landscape that he painted in his studio and another step in his departure from the impressionistic tradition.

Not long after his return to Paris in October he received a visit from a young picture dealer named Daniel Henry Kahnweiler, who had come to Paris at the beginning of the year and in April had opened a small gallery at 28 rue Vignon. Kahnweiler had already bought some work by Picasso, whose "Negro Period" was disliked by the dealers Vollard and Sagot, and he also had acquired a few canvases by Derain, Vlaminck and Van Dongen. Kahnweiler bought the *View from Hotel Mistral* and another recent landscape, a *View of the Viaduct*, showing three high arches (page 25). Soon after this first meeting the young dealer arranged to purchase Braque's entire production.

At the Kahnweiler Gallery Braque frequently saw Picasso and the other young painters in the group. Although he still preferred solitude, he began to join the others at cafés or studios, and to meet some of their friends. It was Guillaume Apollinaire who told Braque about the large composition of nudes which Picasso had been painting for nearly a year, and he took him to see it at the *bateau-lavoir*, where Picasso had his studio. The painting, now entitled *Les Demoiselles d'Avignon*, in the collection of the Museum of Modern Art, represents a group of female nudes, drawn with severe angular contours and planes. It has a powerful impact even today, and must have seemed revolutionary in the fall of 1907 when Braque saw it. According to Fernande Olivier[6], Braque did not like the picture and resisted all the arguments of Picasso in its favor. In December, however, he went to work on a large composition of a standing nude which is unmistakably related to the angular figures of the *Demoiselles*[7] (page 26). The figure has the same emphasis on curves and angles. The background consists of large block-like shapes placed at oblique angles to one another. The color is keyed low in gray, tan and pink, and the modeling is conveyed by bold parallel strokes that give the planes the illusion of tilting back and forth in space. None of these qualities is represented as powerfully as in Picasso's *Demoiselles*. Nevertheless, Braque seems to have grasped the meaning and possibilities of this revolutionary painting.

While Braque was experimenting with these angularities in his large *Nude*, others were abandoning the *fauve* manner. Matisse developed his own style in the large *Joie de Vivre*. Derain ceased painting colorful landscapes and began to work on figure paintings which bore a strong resemblance to Picasso and Cézanne. Vlaminck soon did the same. By the end of 1907, it was evident that the *fauve* movement had spent itself.

2. BRAQUE AND CUBISM (1908-1920)

THE CEZANNE PERIOD

Braque returned to L'Estaque in the spring of 1908. There he began a series of landscapes quite unlike any of his earlier pictures in this region. His palette, now completely divested of the red, blue and violet gamut of *fauvism*, was restricted to ochres and light greens. Carrying still further the trend begun in the *View from Hotel Mistral*, he gave much emphasis to structural lines. Within these outlined areas he painted long parallel strips of hatching, like those in the large *Nude* of the previous winter, setting up a series of planes at angles to the picture surface. As landscape motifs he now selected large-scale architectural details: walls, roof, balustrades and viaduct, which emphasized still more the angularity of his composition. His selection of these motifs calls to mind the Provençal landscapes of Cézanne, and Braque readily acknowledged his source. But like so many of the young painters of the decade, he was driven by a spirit of frenzy that expressed itself in emphasis upon geometric structure and yet failed to reveal anything of the internal quality of the southern landscape that is almost always present in Cézanne's pictures.

Braque's exploitation of the Cézanne surface style exceeded any of the efforts in that direction by Derain or Vlaminck. The L'Estaque landscapes retain even today something of the fervor and exuberance of this youthful period. The *Road near L'Estaque* (page 30) is a close-up view similar to certain Cézannes. A path rises through the woods along a concrete retaining wall which slices across the picture and sets up a disturbing tension between the dynamic diagonals of the trees. The most famous landscape of this series is the *Houses at L'Estaque* (page 31). The group of houses completely loses its domestic character and becomes a pile of huge cubes, like blocks of stone in a quarry, whose angular shapes sweep convulsively across the picture from right to left, against the grain, as it were. It is a picture which begged to be called "cubist" and later was. The color in these landscapes plays a peculiarly negative role, as if Braque were doing penance for his *fauve* excesses and pleading with the spectator to forget the red soil, the

Road near L'Estaque, 1908. Oil on canvas, 23¾ x 19¾". Collection the Museum of Modern Art, New York

pines and the blue sky, and to see only volumes in space. This plea is quite characteristic of a generation which was now trying to rid itself of the habits of painting vague, structureless studies of light that were bequeathed to it by the Impressionist school, and was beginning to circulate such statements as Cézanne's famous remark: "Everything in nature is formed according to the sphere, the cone and the cylinder." The urge for expression of geometric volumes in space, at the expense of all other pictorial material, is quite clearly shown in this group of Braque landscapes, and when he exhibited them in Paris a few months later they made a sensation.

By now Braque felt enough confidence in his painting to submit several pictures to the jury of the *Salon d'Automne* of 1908. The jury refused them. However, according to the custom of this *Salon*, each member of the jury had the right to retrieve one picture from a rejected group. Albert Marquet

Houses at L'Estaque, 1908. Oil on canvas, 28¾ x 23⅝". Collection Hermann Rupf, Berne, Switzerland

and Charles Guerin each voted in one of the rejected Braques. When the artist heard of this partial success he was furious, and although he had not the legal right to do so, removed all seven of the paintings.[8]

Henri Matisse, then an officer of the *Salon d'Automne*, is said to have described one of the refused pictures as being made of *"petits cubes"* making a little sketch of it to show to friends. The picture in question is doubtless the *Houses at L'Estaque* referred to above.[9] Matisse, who has been asked about this story hundreds of times, now denies any memory of it and argues, quite rightly, that the legend and the words are utterly superficial and have nothing to do with the school of painting.

Early in November, Henry Kahnweiler arranged a Braque exhibition at his gallery with about forty canvases including the seven rejected pictures. Guillaume Apollinaire wrote the introduction to the catalog and in so doing, went on record as the apostle of modern painting in Paris.

The art critic, Louis Vauxcelles, who had adopted the word *"fauve"* several years earlier, wrote the following paragraph on the exhibition in *Gil Blas*, November 14, 1908: "Braque is a very bold young man. The striking examples set by Derain and Picasso have encouraged him. Perhaps also he has been too much obsessed by the style of Cézanne and his memories of the static art of the Egyptians. He constructs metallic and deformed figures which have a terrible oversimplification. He mistreats form, reduces everything, sites, figures and houses to geometric outlines, to *cubes*. But since he is working in good faith, let us not make fun of him. Let us wait and see."

Braque, who had been practically unknown before his exhibition in the *Salon des Indépendants* of 1907 now achieved the reputation of being one of the young men to watch in *avant-garde* painting. An interesting contrast to the Vauxcelles paragraph on Braque is one written two months later by Guillaume Apollinaire,[10] probably referring to the large *Nude* mentioned above:

Visibly [Braque] proceeds from a geometric *a priori* to which the entire field of his vision is submitted and he attempts to translate the whole thing by combinations of a few absolute forms. Before his paintings of women people have cried out in horror: "hideous, monstrous!" That sort of remark is spoken too hastily. Where we think we are looking for a feminine figure because the catalogue reads "female nude" the artist has seen only geometric harmonies which for him are a complete expression of nature. For him this female figure was merely a pretext for containing those harmonies in certain lines, and putting them into relation with certain tonalities. In these three realms he searches equally and uniquely for these harmonies. No one was less concerned than he with the psychology of his subject and I believe a stone would move him as much as a face. He has created a new personal alphabet of which each character has universal acceptance. Before declaring it to be a hideous grimace tell me if you have really grasped it, if you have understood the decorative intentions.

33

Still Life with Musical Instruments, 1908. Oil on canvas, 19¾ x 24⅛". Owned by the artist

TOWARD CUBISM

During the time he painted the Cézannesque landscapes, Braque did one or two still lifes in this same tonality of light green and ochre. One of these (above), seems to him to have special significance for two reasons: it consists of a group of musical instruments, and it is painted entirely from the imagination instead of from life. In his gradual emancipation from the concept of impressionism, Braque began to develop a free visual imagination. He had already started with the two landscapes done in the fall of 1907. The still life is another step of the progression.

The early date of this still life seems to prove that it was Braque who introduced the theme of musical instruments into the iconography of cubism. Before long, he was to paint a whole repertory of musical subjects: guitar players, mandolin players, still-life compositions with these and other instruments such as the flute or violin, as well as sheet music, notes, clefs and bars.

In spite of what Guillaume Apollinaire may have thought about the artist's indifference to subject matter, it is evident that there is some connection here to Braque's fondness for music. Some critics have suggested that there is a symbolical meaning to be found in the repertory of cubist

34

Port in Normandy, 1909. Oil on canvas, 32 x 32". Collection Walter P. Chrysler, Jr., Warrenton, Virginia

subject matter, not only the musical instruments but also the bottles and glasses, pipes, tobacco and newspapers. Juan Gris remarked, although perhaps jokingly, that in the guitar Braque had found a new Madonna. On the other hand, it is well to remember that several of these objects have shapes that readily suggest spheres, cylinders or variations on geometric forms.

35

Still Life with Fruit Dish, 1908. Oil on canvas, 20⅞ x 25⅟₁₆". Collection Rolf de Maré, Stockholm

In the early spring of 1909, Braque painted a large square canvas entitled *Port in Normandy* (page 35). Done from the imagination, it represents two fishing boats entering a harbor whose breakwaters appear in the immediate background. The twin entrance towers and the ships' hulls are modeled in bold relief. The waves, sails and sky break up into small tilting planes, and the spars fill the center with opposing vertical and diagonal lines. The colors are dark and gloomy, and an eerie light flows in from the right side. Braque must have had in his imagination a violent Channel storm, of the sort that Turner painted, but the dynamic force of the storm is converted into a struggle of semi-abstract volumes. Whereas Turner played on the emotions we associate with the experience of a storm, Braque almost entirely eliminates such associations. The ships, breakwaters, seas and sky become objects whose only name and connotation is volume, angle, plane, diagonal, etc. Yet they have meaning and value and even arouse an emotional feeling in the spectator.

During the same period he painted one or two still lifes with fruit, such as the one illustrated above. The compote dish is fluted like a melon, the fruit spreads out to the edges of the canvas, and the rounded volumes of

36

pears and apples become angular and seem to crowd one another in filling the space.

Braque exhibited the large *Port* and a similar fruit-bowl still life (since destroyed) at the *Salon des Indépendants* that spring where, according to André Salmon, they made a sensation. Louis Vauxcelles, who had used the term "cube" in writing of Braque's November exhibition, wrote of these two landscapes as "*bizarreries cubiques.*"[11] This was to be Braque's last *Salon* appearance for thirteen years. The group of painters at the Kahnweiler Gallery, having found the public and the critics increasingly hostile to its work, decided to stop sending pictures to the various *Salons* and to exhibit only at Kahnweiler's.

THE GROUP AT MONTMARTRE

The painters of the gallery were brought closer by this withdrawal from the *Salons*. They exhibited together and their pictures were bought by a small group of collectors—Hermann Rupf, Roger Dutilleul, Wilhelm Uhde and others. The derision of the press and public caused them to band together in self-defense. This attitude may have been reinforced by the social backgrounds of the artists. Neither Picasso nor Braque had ever lived an upper-middle-class life, as Manet and Degas had. At that time their earnings were quite modest and both lived in Montmartre in the traditional Bohemian manner.

His friends from these years remember Braque as being tall, though not as tall as Derain, heavily built, with a powerful almost negroid head, dark complexion and curly hair. Both he and Derain were skilled boxers. Like Vlaminck, Braque often affected vulgar speech and Parisian argot. He dressed in blue work clothes which he wore with a certain swagger, as he does to this day. His dress, whether in studio clothes or for the street, was a discreet blend of elegance and studied carelessness. Although born in a Parisian suburb, he was usually thought of as a Norman, like Dufy and Friesz, and was considered to have the traits of character traditionally attributed to the Norman peasant. Apollinaire once described him as "the celebrated Cubist, illustrious accordion player and reformer of costume... as well as pastmaster of the dance." Henri Laurens tells how Braque used to play the accordion with feeling and dignity. Braque has long professed a love for the music of Bach, Rameau and Couperin, and possibly he identifies certain aspects of their music with qualities he wishes to express in his painting.

Picasso and Juan Gris were then living at the *bateau-lavoir* on rue Ravignan. Max Jacob lived nearby. They used to eat at the Restaurant

Pablo Picasso: Portrait of Braque, 1909. Oil on canvas, 24¼ x 19¾". Collection Edward A. Bragaline

Azon on rue Ravignan, a cheap place patronized by coachmen and masons. Guillaume Apollinaire would come regularly, often bringing Marie Laurencin. Vlaminck and Derain joined them occasionally, as did Braque. Gertrude and Leo Stein were also friends of the group. Nearly every week the groups would go to the performance at the *Cirque Medrano* where Picasso was delighted by the clowns. Many of them attended the poetry discussion held on Tuesday evenings at the *Closerie des Lilas*, on the left bank. They were all present at the famous banquet organized for Henri Rousseau.

It will be noted that there were as many writers as artists in this group of friends at Montmartre. Picasso had known Max Jacob since 1902. He met Guillaume Apollinaire in 1905, and Gertrude Stein the same year. Braque met Maurice Raynal in 1904; later he became friendly with Blaise Cendrars and Pierre Reverdy. Apollinaire wrote understandingly of these artists in the press and in his own review *Les Soirées de Paris*. Kahnweiler encouraged these friendships by asking Apollinaire to write the preface for Braque's exhibition and by publishing books of Max Jacob and Apollinaire with illustrations by artists in his gallery. The stimulations which resulted from the frequent meetings between these poets and painters was an important factor in the development of cubism, particularly in the discussions of theory and the formulation of cubist esthetics.

PICASSO AND BRAQUE

About 1909 Picasso and Braque became close friends and in the years that followed they developed a partnership of mutual exchange of artistic ideas that is rare, if not unique in the history of art. Henry Kahnweiler remembers how the two young artists used to drop into his gallery day after day. Picasso would usually call for Braque about five when it was too dark to paint any longer, and they would walk down the hill from Montmartre to the rue Vignon back of the Madeleine. There in the back room of the gallery they used to discuss their painting and many other subjects. Often Derain and other painters of the gallery would join these gatherings.

In a year or two Picasso and Braque began painting pictures which were sometimes so similar that their friends could distinguish one from the other only with great difficulty. Once, many years later, Picasso sat for a long time studying what he took to be one of his cubist pictures in the Doucet Collection before he finally discovered, from the signature on the back, that it had been painted by Braque.

The psychological aspects of this relationship will perhaps never be fully

Head of a Woman, 1909. Oil on canvas. Collection Dr. Girardin, Paris

Pitcher, Bottle and Lemon, 1909. Oil on canvas, 18⅛ x 15".
Present owner unknown

Guitar and Compote Dish, 1909. Oil on canvas, 28¾ x 23⅝",
Collection Hermann Rupf, Berne, Switzerland

known, particularly since their friendship has long since lost its fervor and neither will speak readily of their mutual past. Today they seem so different that one wonders how this interchange could have lasted as long as it did; Picasso, passionate, forceful, restless; Braque, reserved, measured, almost shy. They seem as unlike as van Gogh and Gauguin. Obviously these differences were less marked in their youth when both were quite evidently driven by some mutual mysterious inner force.

Today we can perceive vital differences in their artistic production, even though there are a number of paintings that may confuse the connoisseurs of the future. A cubist painting by Picasso is apt to emphasize the drawing and the illusion of plastic quality. One by Braque is usually rich in textural qualities and delicate in color and line. Often its composition will seem calm when compared to a Picasso, and there will be a sense of elegance and restraint.

These differences can be discovered in most of their paintings of the cubist period, and they give us at least a hint of the roles played by the two men. Picasso was surely, as he is today, more forceful, more varied, and in so far as the purely plastic element of cubism is concerned, more signifi-

40

La Roche-Guyon with Tower, 1909. Oil on canvas, 28¾ x 23⅝". Collection Roger Dutilleul, Paris

cant. But Braque was much more than a mere follower. True, he had an extraordinary ability to assimilate pictorial ideas that may have originated with Picasso, but he understood the real meaning and aim of cubism and participated in its revolutionary development. In his own right as the co-inventor of cubism, Braque was a supreme technician in the handling of paint, a resourceful yet sustained innovator and an extremely sensitive and subtle decorator. Above all he had a genius for achieving a sense of internal order and discipline that gave a sense of permanence to the most casual images.

41

Still Life with Violin and Pitcher, 1909-10. Oil on canvas, 46½ x 28¾". Private collection,
Paris

View from the Artist's Studio, 1910. Oil on canvas, 21⅝ x 16⅛". Collection Roger Dutilleul, Paris

During that summer of 1909, Picasso was in Spain at Horta de Ebro near Tolosa, where he did a number of landscapes which resemble Braque's to the extent that they emphasize geometric volumes, but Picasso's colors were deep red and brown, his representation of volumes very forceful and dynamic. Braque spent the summer at La Roche-Guyon on the Seine near Mantes. The picturesque little village is dominated by an ancient castle which rises steeply toward the cliffs above the river. Braque made several landscapes, imaginatively composed from the architecture of the village, particularly the castle. He used its tower as a central motif around which he arranged the masses of houses and trees in such a way as to suggest a

43

Still Life with Guitar, 1909-10. Oil on canvas, 28¾ x 23⅝". Private collection, England

vigorous upward movement. Often he introduced a tall tree trunk at one side of the picture, a device to reinforce the structure of his composition and probably borrowed from Cézanne. The color is rather similar to the pale ochres and greens of the L'Estaque series, but the composition in the best of the La Roche-Guyon landscapes (page 41) is more subtle in the handling of planes. Later in the year he painted some landscapes at Carrières St. Denis, where he went with Derain. These are in the same style as the La Roche-Guyon pictures.

44

Woman with a Mandolin, 1910. Oil on canvas, 36 x 28½". Collection Walter P. Chrysler, Jr., Warrenton, Virginia

The Portuguese, 1911. Oil on canvas, 46¼ x 28¾". Private collection, Paris

Man with a Guitar, 1911. Oil on canvas, 45¾ x 31⅞". Collection the Museum of Modern Art, New York. Acquired through the Lillie P. Bliss Bequest

47

The Match Holder, 1910. Oil on canvas, 13¾ x 10⅝". Collection Roger Dutilleul, Paris

ANALYTICAL CUBISM

Like most terms applied to the visual arts, "analytical" is not very exact yet it does describe in a general way the cubist process of taking apart or breaking down the forms of nature. "Analytical" also conveys something of the spirit of investigation and dissection of form carried on by Picasso and Braque almost as if their studios were laboratories.[12]   ALFRED H. BARR, JR.

In 1909 Picasso painted a *Portrait of Braque* (page 38) which, although it has not the likeness of his 1910 portrait of Kahnweiler, is a good example of the effort to break the surface into a composition of angular planes or facets. Braque's *Head of a Woman* (page 39), also painted in 1909, was done in the same spirit, if not with the same effect.

In the still-life paintings of 1909 one can observe what appears to be a progression towards a more determined geometric treatment of shapes. The *Pitcher, Bottle and Lemon* (page 40), done during the summer, represents these objects on a square table whose top tilts downward to create the illusion of shallow picture space. The pitcher is heavily modeled with only a suggestion of angularity. The contour of the bottle is repeated on one side

48

but otherwise its form is intact. In the *Guitar and Compote Dish* (page 40), presumably painted in the autumn, there is a similar tilted table top but the objects are distributed in the picture space with restless animation. The guitar appears to be propped up on a diagonal axis. The vigorous parallel brush strokes set up a series of indefinite planes within the objects which make the composition restless and unstable.

At the end of the year 1909 Braque began work on a large vertical canvas, (probably not completed until the spring of 1910) the most ambitious and successful up to that point in his career: *Still Life with Violin and Pitcher* (page 42). The colors are mostly olive green and gray with reddish brown on the violin. The picture space is again suggested by a tilt-top table, but here it rises almost vertically and the depth behind it is immediately shut off by a series of walls and panels. The principal objects, a large pitcher and a violin, are recognizable without difficulty. The handsome curves of the violin make a pleasing contrast with their bristling rectilinear environment. They seem to have been crystallized into a large-faceted block which rises like a multi-surfaced pyramid to the top of the picture. There one discovers a curiously incongruous detail—a large nail, with a cast shadow, as if it fastened the canvas to the wall.

The transposition of solid shapes into faceted surfaces is seen in several of Braque's canvases of 1909-10, such as the *Still Life with Guitar* (page 44). This runs parallel to similar work by Picasso and is an important phase in the progression of analytical cubism. But the nail was an innovation that caused much discussion among Braque, Picasso and their friends. Kahnweiler argued that this revealed a new significance in their painting.[13] It was held to be a sudden evocation of reality, in the midst of their bold departure from material appearances. Now that we can see not only what preceded, but also what followed, it appears as a logical step toward later developments in cubism.

In the spring of 1910 Braque painted a view from his studio window on the top floor of the rue d'Orsel, where he could look up across the rooftops at the white domes of Sacré-Coeur (page 43). The subject, which is almost entirely limited to architectural detail, has more uniformity of geometric shape than the landscapes of La Roche-Guyon and there is less tension, more tranquility. The colors are gray, beige, black and white. Deep space in the traditional sense is deliberately suppressed and the buildings, whether far or near, hover upon the surface of the canvas.

That summer, Braque went once more to L'Estaque. Kahnweiler visited him there in September and the artist pointed out the sites from which he had painted some of his landscapes in 1908, such as the *Houses at L'Estaque*. Kahnweiler was astonished at their fidelity to natural details in the landscape. However, by 1910 Braque, like Picasso, was painting entirely from invention and imagination. He once remarked to a friend that some of his best pictures had been composed while he was reclining on his studio couch.

49

Battleship, 1910-11. Oil on canvas, 31½ x 23″. Private collection

Soda, 1911. Oil on canvas, 14¼" diameter. Collection the Museum of Modern Art, New York. Acquired through the Lillie P. Bliss Bequest

That summer Braque worked on still-life subjects more than on landscapes although he did do two paintings suggested by the Rio Tinto factory buildings near Marseilles.

At about that time, or possibly a little earlier, he began to use oval canvases; perhaps he found that the curve made a pleasing contrast to the angular shapes within, or perhaps a further variation upon the play of curves in some of the still-life objects: guitars, violins, goblets. He also began a series of paintings on the motif of a half-length figure with musical instrument, a subject that Picasso was then doing at Cadaqués. The figure is rigorously broken down into angular and circular planes (page 45). The female body and the musical instrument merge into a single volume in space as if they were unconsciously inter-related in the artist's mind.

51

Still Life with Grapes, 1912. Oil and sand on canvas, 23⅝ x 28¾". Galerie Louise Léiris, Paris

The superposition of planes which appears in Picasso's work that summer is not particularly noticeable in Braque's and we may assume that Braque assimilated this important phase of cubism at a slightly later date. The same may be said of the related idea of introducing overlapping planes from a multiple point of view. This does not appear in Braque's work as frequently as in Picasso's. In contrast to Picasso's passionate and restless search for means to express volumes moving in space, Braque seems to have been more concerned with the development of surface, of texture and of new relationships with reality.

In the spring of 1911 Braque made another in his series of figure paintings; this one (page 46), he called *The Portuguese,* after a guitar player he had seen at a bar in Marseilles. The colors of beige, tan and black are much the same as those Picasso was using at the time. The facet surfaces have now become a complex group of short straight lines and arcs which ebb and flow swiftly in a shallow picture space. But this serene world of formal harmonies is rudely interrupted by a group of stencilled letters and numbers. This is the first appearance of these irrelevant and conspicuous symbols which were later so widely used.

What is their meaning? Looking back into Braque's previous paintings one finds an occasional example of lettering such as the *Gil Blas* newspaper in a small painting of 1910, *The Match Holder* (page 48) or the letters on a book cover in another still life of that year, but in these earlier pictures the letters are represented as casual details in a semi-impressionistic manner. Braque had known how to do hand lettering since his apprentice days, but the sudden appearance of these letters in the midst of a cubist composition can only be explained as another attempt to evoke reality—like the *trompe l'oeil* nail. It might be compared to the introduction of mechanical sounds into music, or advertising slogans into poetry. In addition to the shock value of the irrelevant BAL & 10, 40, there is also a decorative effect, and these letters were to be much used for this purpose by Picasso, Gris and most of all by Braque himself.

One need hardly add that they have influenced subsequent advertising design, and have also vastly enriched our own visual experiences by opening our eyes to similar designs in casual and unexpected places. In two of his recent paintings Braque has again used the printed letter, as printing on the side of a packing case.

The sculptor Manolo, a friend of Picasso's, lived at Céret, a small town on the French side of the Pyrenees and at his suggestion several of the group decided to spend the summer of 1911 there. This produced such a flourishing of new painting that Maurice Raynal later called Céret the "Barbizon of Cubism." Picasso and Fernande, among the first to arrive, had rented a house. Braque and Marcelle Lapré found an apartment nearby. The paintings of both artists now developed such a shallow depth that the volumes, instead of receding, gave the illusion of rising like relief sculpture away from a background that remained close to the surface of the canvas. Because of its crowded, shut-off space, this was sometimes called "hermetic cubism."

One of Braque's most forceful compositions of the summer was the *Man with a Guitar* (page 47). Composed of arcs, acute angles, half cylinders and scrolls, it is contained by a series of long straight lines and crossing diagonals, which rise in a massive pyramid against a flat ground. An odd loop of rope at one side seems to offer itself to one's grasp and, like the nail, is another evocation of reality. The color is severe tan and gray with a touch here and there of blue green enriched by a texture of short brush strokes, a sort of severe neo-impressionism. In its purity, order and severity one will perhaps be reminded of certain musical compositions for strings.

Another development of this period was a series of pictures with similar scrolls, acute angles and curvilinear volumes, but executed with a broader, sketchier line and with detail so crowded that it pushes out to the edge of the picture. A good example of this is the oval composition nicknamed *Battleship* (page 50) and the small circular painting (page 51) of a glass, a pipe and the letters SODA. Many of the paintings of these years used letters as in a small rectangular canvas of 1912 entitled *The Kubelick Poster*.

53

*Fruit Bowl, 1912. Pasted paper and charcoal on paper, 24⁷⁄₁₆ x 18⁷⁄₈".
Present owner unknown*

SCHOOL OF CUBISM

Braque returned to Paris in October. For a short time during that year he had a studio on the Impasse Guelma, near the Place Pigalle. Picasso was living at 11 Boulevard de Clichy. Sometimes he and Fernande would join Braque and Marcelle at the *Lapin à Gill.* The group of friends remained about the same, but several other artists had begun to paint in the cubist manner. Best known of these was Fernand Léger, who had been painting in this style since 1910, but he lived on the left bank and rarely came to Montmartre.

Cubism first drew public attention as a new school of painting during the year 1911. Now that the movement had acquired a group of followers and imitators, the term had gradually come into usage. Gallery 41 at the *Salon des Indépendants* that spring had included paintings by Delaunay, Gleizes,

54

Still Life with Playing Cards, 1913. Gouache and pasted paper on canvas, 31½ x 23¼". Collection the Musée National d'Art Moderne, Paris

de la Fresnaye, Lhote and Metzinger. In October the *Salon d'Automne* gave a special gallery to the cubists including Léger, Jacques Villon and several of those who had shown at the *Salon des Indépendants*. Ironically enough, Picasso and Braque, the founders of cubism, abstained from both exhibitions.

Neither Braque nor Picasso had any idea of forming a school of painting. Of this question Braque had said, "Cubism or rather my cubism was a means that I created for my use, whose primary aim was to put painting within the reach of my own gifts . . . ." And Picasso is quoted by Christian Zervos as saying, "When we made cubism we had no intention of making cubism but of expressing what was in us . . . ." Perhaps that was the reason why both men ignored the group of cubist followers. They did, however, admire the work of Juan Gris who began to develop his own cubism this same year.

Black and White Collage, 1913. Pasted paper, charcoal and white chalk on paper, 24½ x 18⅛". Collection Miss Katherine S. Dreier, Milford, Connecticut

Collage with Newspaper, 1912. Pasted paper and pencil on board, 28¼ x 39¾". Buchholz Gallery, New York

In the summer of 1912 Picasso returned to Céret, where Gris and others joined him. At the end of July he left suddenly and going to Avignon he discovered the nearby town of Sorgues where he settled down to paint and invited Braque, who was still in Paris, to join him. Braque accepted at once and rented a small house called *Villa Bel Air*. The house had an attic large enough to serve as a studio. Braque had been fond of the *Midi* for years and Sorgues seemed to suit him particularly well. He was to return there for many summers. Once he even made the journey from Paris by bicycle.

It is generally agreed that the so-called analytical period of cubism reached an end about this time—although there are "analytical" canvases by Braque as late as 1913. But many of Braque's paintings of 1912 seem to have originated in a different way. As Gris put it, "from a cylinder I make

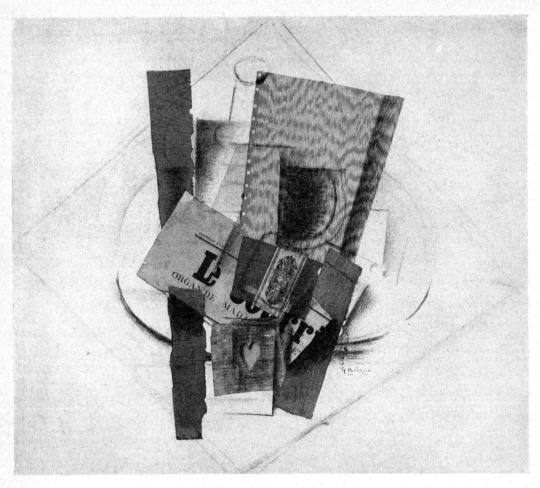

Le Courrier, 1913. Pasted paper on board, 20 x 22½". Courtesy Mr. Gallatin: A. E. Gallatin Collection, The Philadelphia Museum of Art

a bottle." This implied reversal of direction should be accepted only with reservations. Nevertheless there is an evident search for the synthesis in much of Braque's work of 1912 and 1913.

During this first stay at Sorgues he began experimenting with sand and other foreign materials mixed into the oil pigment. An early example of this technique is the *Still Life with Grapes* with the letters SORG[UES] (page 52). Both Picasso and Braque felt dissatisfied with the possibilities of the oil medium and the limitations it imposed. For three or four years they had rejected nearly all color and had been producing paintings of almost monochromatic effect. The introduction of sand was another step in Braque's evocation of reality. At some time during the year he introduced bits of green or gray marbleized surfaces into some of his pictures and also rec-

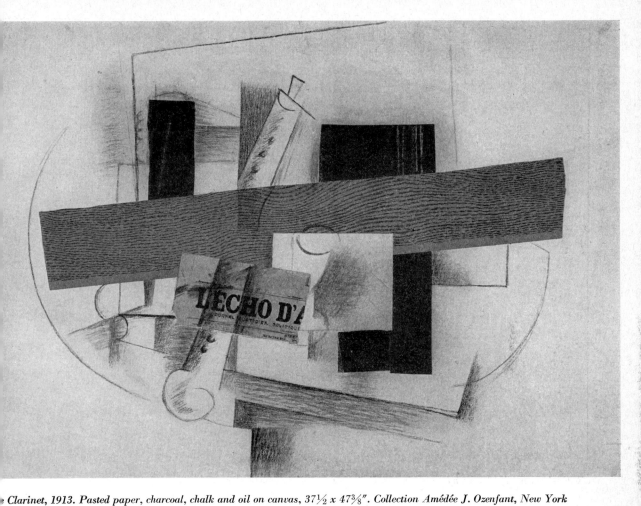

Clarinet, 1913. Pasted paper, charcoal, chalk and oil on canvas, 37½ x 47⅜". Collection Amédée J. Ozenfant, New York

tangular strips painted in imitation of wood grain.

A great deal has been written about the sources of these devices in his commercial painting apprenticeship. However, he had been painting for twelve years before they appeared in his work. It is significant that none of them appears in his paintings of the *fauve* or Cézanne periods. The new attitude toward painting which was then developing out of cubist theories and experiments gave Braque this opportunity to draw upon his past experience. First it had been the *trompe l'oeil* nail, then the block lettering, and now marbleizing and wood graining. In retrospect, this sequence appears to be logical and perhaps inevitable. Nevertheless, it was a happy chance that the otherwise unrelated phenomena of house-painting conventions and a new theory of representing volumes in space were to join as

59

Musical Forms, 1913. Oil and pasted paper. Collection Mr. and Mrs. Walter C. Arensberg, Hollywood

formative elements in Braque's painting of these years. It brought about a new and rich phase in the maturing of his own style and led directly to some of his great post-war paintings.

THE COLLAGES

Who made the first collage? This is a question which will never find a satisfactory answer unless it is stated in the same evolutionary terms. For it was in this atmosphere of cubist theory and under the same impulses that the first papier collés or collages were made. Picasso, whose extraordinary talent and passion make him as much a draftsman as a painter, and as much a sculptor as a draftsman, had many times experimented with sculpture. At that moment he had been experimenting with painted metal and

60

Guitar, 1913-14. Oil on canvas with pasted paper, pencil and chalk, 39¼ x 25⅝". Collection the Museum of Modern Art, New York. Acquired through the Lillie P. Bliss Bequest

61

Collage, 1913. Pasted paper and crayon on canvas. Collection Pablo Picasso, Paris

possibly other materials. Braque in the meantime had been making paper
sculpture, folding it into shapes like certain geometric details in his paintings. None of these has survived but we can guess what they looked like
from the fact that Picasso in a letter of that date addressed Braque as "*Mon
vieux Vilbure*," referring to Wilbur Wright. These paper sculptures seem to
have suggested possible adaptations to painting which led to the making
of the first collage.

As Braque remembers it, this was at Sorgues in September of 1912.
Picasso had already returned to Paris. He and Marcelle stayed on at the
Villa Bel Air. His eye was attracted by some wallpaper at an Avignon shop,
printed to resemble the close grain of quartered oak. He bought some,
took it to the studio and began experimenting with it. The first composi-

62

Glass and Violin, 1912. Pasted paper and oil on canvas, 45¾ x 31⅞". Private collection, Paris

tion he made with this papier collé or glued-on paper, was on a sheet of drawing paper about two feet high, upon which he pasted the strips of the wood-grain paper (page 54). He then drew a simple composition in charcoal. He sketched a bunch of grapes, a goblet, and beneath the grapes a suggestion of a compote dish upon a table. One of the strips was placed at the bottom where it suggests the table drawer. Another was neatly cut out to fit the curve of the fruit bowl. The drawing was extended across some of the pasted strips and the letters ALE and BAR were added.[14]

Soon Braque made other collages, at first preferring to use only black strips, as in the *Black and White Collage* (page 56). Later he added newspaper, sometimes cutting it into the shape of a guitar (page 57). Picasso was quick to follow the device; indeed it is possible he may already have produced collages in material other than paper.

Braque, then, made the first papier collé, but who knows what discussions preceded it, what mutual ideas and inspiration, what forgotten remarks or sketches led up to the discovery?

In many of the first collages the drawn details are in black and white, in short, they are drawings with pasted paper, but others combine strips of newspaper and various other papers. Later many of Braque's collages are composed on large rectangular boards or canvases which have been sized and painted flat white, as the spacious and graceful *Clarinet* (page 59). *Le Courrier* (page 58) is a good example of a design with varied materials: grained paper, newspaper headline, cigarette package and clipping. A more complex design is achieved in the oval *Collage* (page 62) belonging to Picasso, which includes part of a handbill from the *Tivoli-Cinema* at Sorgues, with the evocative words "*Statue d'Epouvante.*"

If some of Braque's oil paintings of 1910 and 1911 bear a close resemblance to the work of Picasso, the collages have qualities particularly his own, which can be recognized at once by comparison with the collages of Picasso or Gris. Those of Picasso achieve plastic form, an illusion of volume in space, together with an arresting tension. A collage by Gris is usually rich in color, with contrasting light and dark areas. The most successful by Braque achieve a sense of elegance and serenity as in *The Clarinet*. The musical instruments and wine glasses have a kind of cardboard reality like playing cards; these thin, delicate shapes appear to hover over the surface in a boundless white space. One of the finest examples of this quality is the vertical composition with three or four strips of colored paper which is infinitely subtle in its illusion of floating movement (page 61). It might be mentioned that in this example the cut-out paper has not greatly changed with age; whereas the yellowing of the newspaper in many collages has created an entirely different inter-relationship of planes, which was doubtless not anticipated by the artists. Braque also made a few collages with cut-out shapes in papers of various textures and colors with very little added drawing (page 60).

Still Life on Table, 1913. Oil on canvas, 23⅝ x 28¾". Private collection, Paris

CUBIST PAINTING, 1913-1914

Both Braque and Picasso made use of their visual discoveries in collage to develop new designs in their painting. The *trompe l'oeil* device, which Braque had introduced several years earlier was now used in painting facsimiles of cigarette packages, sheets of music and strips of grained wood, as in the *Still Life with Playing Cards* of 1913 (page 55) or the oval *Glass and Violin* (page 63). The device of floating planes suggested in earlier cubist paintings, and developed with the collages, now appeared in oil paintings such as the *Musical Score* (page 66).

The complex and crowded compositions of 1911 and 1912 do not entirely disappear after the collage; one of Braque's most forceful cubist paintings

Musical Score, 1913. Oil on canvas, 25⅝ x 36¼″. Private collection, Paris

is the oval *Still Life on Table*, 1913 (page 65). The colors are beige and gray with black, the objects: pipe, sheet music, guitar and letters on a round table with open drawer, are seen in tilting and overlapping planes but in a space which is less crowded than the "hermetic" compositions.

Cubism continued to gain fame during these years. The group called the *Section d'Or*, founded in the studio of Jacques Villon, held its first exhibition in October, 1912. Gris exhibited with them. That year also cubism began to be seen abroad at the *Sonderbund* in Cologne, the Grafton Gallery in London and the *Moderne Kunst* group in Amsterdam. Picasso's pictures were bringing prices up to four thousand francs. Braque, who was less known, and still thought by many to be a follower of Picasso, obtained prices of about four hundred francs.

Braque and his wife, Marcelle, spent the summer of 1913 at *Villa Bel Air*, Sorgues. In mid-autumn he returned to Paris, and to his studio in the

Woman with Guitar, 1913. Oil on canvas, 51¼ x 29⅛″. Private collection, Paris,

67

Composition with Letters JOH, 1914. Pasted paper and crayon on paper, 16¾ x 27". Collection Marius de Zayas, Stamford, Connecticut

Hotel Roma, 101 rue Caulaincourt. Perhaps the culminating picture in this fruitful year is the large vertical canvas *Woman with Guitar* (page 67). The tans and gray greens are now enhanced by several broad areas of imitation wood grain in cinnamon brown; the sheet music and letters SO[N]ATE are shuffled with a newspaper headline. The angular planes are broader and less tense than those in his guitar players of 1911.

Cubism of 1914 entered into a *détente*, a state of relaxation from the severe and sober paintings of 1911. The period of research and discovery became one of refinement. Both in his paintings and collages Braque used a little more color and ornament. The *Composition with Letters* JOH (above) is a good example of this decorative quality. One of the most delightful paintings of 1914 is the *Oval Still Life* (opposite). Braque has composed a

68

Oval Still Life (Le violon), *1914. Oil on canvas, 36⅜ x 25¾". Collection the Museum of Modern Art, New York. Gift of the Advisory Committee*

69

Drawing, 1912? Present owner unknown

group of paper-thin rectangular planes suggesting parts of a violin, sheet music, wallpaper design and molding. The colors are blue and tan and the tonality very pale and delicate. Around the outside of the oval and at various internal edges there are shaded areas which give the illusion of lifting the planes up from the background so that they seem to hover in mid-air, floating gracefully and elegantly in this imagined space. Even in his drawing there is a less insistent spirit of analysis. The contour lines are less rectilinear, more curvilinear.

The most striking painting in this new manner is *Music,* a still life with a violin, glass and pipe (opposite). The surface is more richly varied in texture and color. The sandy planes of warm tan are surrounded by areas dotted in blue gray. The forms are as clean and bold as a fresco, yet they are contained by an oddly misshapen oval that is entirely different from the geometric curves hitherto used. This is one of the earliest instances of the free curve that Arp and others were to employ after the war.

70

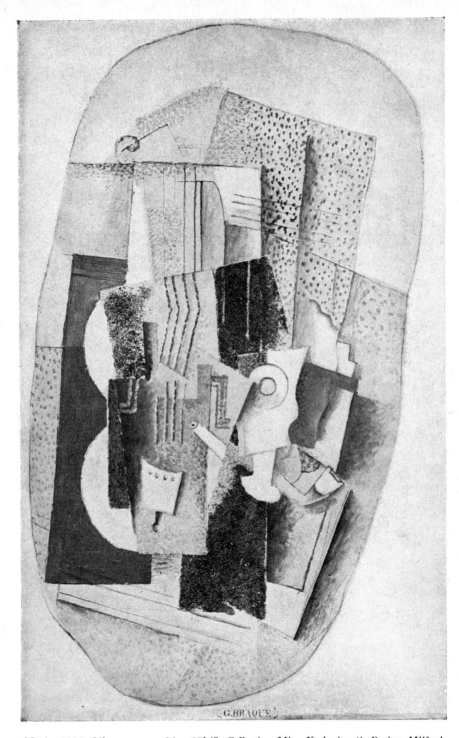

Music, 1914. Oil on canvas, 36 x 23½". Collection Miss Katherine S. Dreier, Milford, Connecticut

71

In the summer of 1914 Braque had just arrived at Sorgues and begun to paint when the war broke out. He received his orders for mobilization immediately and, leaving his wife at Sorgues, he went to Paris. Derain, who had been at Avignon with Picasso, left with him.

Braque joined his regiment at Amiens with the rank of sergeant. By September he was at the front and in December was promoted to a lieutenancy. On May 11, 1915, at Carency on the Artois sector of the front, Braque was severely wounded in the head by an exploding shell. He was given a trepanning operation in a field hospital at the front. A month later he was sent to Paris, where he remained in the hospital for several months. Just after he arrived in June, 1915, Juan Gris visited him and wrote to Kahnweiler that poor Braque was still in serious danger. For a time Braque lost his eyesight, but gradually he recovered and was sent back to his regiment as

The Goblet, 1917-18. Oil on cardboard, 24 x 18". Courtesy Mr. Gallatin: A. E. Gallatin Collection, The Philadelphia Museum of Art

Woman with a Mandolin, 1917. Oil on canvas, 36¼ x 25⅝". Collection Roger Dutilleul, Paris

a convalescent in April, 1916. He was mustered out a few months later and was able to join his wife at their apartment at 11 rue Simon Dereure, in Paris. For his acts of courage and sacrifice, Braque was awarded two citations, the *Croix de Guerre* and the *Legion d'Honneur*.

73

The war broke up the group of poets and painters who had created the atmosphere of cubism. Picasso and Juan Gris were Spanish nationals and continued to live in France and paint, as did a few of the French artists who were not eligible for military service. Braque, Apollinaire, Derain and Marcoussis were in the French Army. The Kahnweiler Gallery was closed; Henry Kahnweiler, although married to a Frenchwoman, was a German citizen, and he had gone to Switzerland. Cubist painting continued, but some of those who observed the movement both before and after the war felt that the revolutionary spirit, the youth and passion, had gone, and with it much of the promise of a renaissance in contemporary art.

Braque and Picasso were now separated. They had a personal quarrel just before the war, and have remained somewhat distant ever since.

After spending the summer of 1917 at Sorgues, Braque returned in the fall to his old studio on the top floor of the Hotel Roma, at 101 rue Caulaincourt. After three years of absence he found it difficult to take up where he left off. Picasso was in Italy working with the *Ballets Russes*. Braque was glad to see Juan Gris, and he liked Gris's recent paintings. Guillaume Apollinaire was back in Paris after suffering from a head wound which was to cause his death in November, 1918. Gradually Braque was able to recover some of the forgotten past.

His first important painting after the war was the *Woman with a Mandolin* (page 73) completed in the fall of 1917. It is designed in broad flat planes and, although low in key, is more colorful than any canvas since his *fauve* period. Areas of green, yellow and dull red harmonize with the background grays. A panel of white dots on tan resembles his paintings of 1914, but otherwise there is much difference. The planes give no illusion of tilting or floating; instead they fit together flatly like a picture puzzle with only one or two suggestions of depth. The easy compass curves around the head and shoulders, the stylized curves of the hands and mandolin bear such a strong resemblance to the figure painting Juan Gris was doing in 1916 and 1917 that we may conclude that Braque adopted this style as a means of guiding his return to current cubist painting. However, comparison with a contemporary figure painting by Gris shows that Braque has transposed the color scheme and design so that they almost become his own style.

Braque also began to experiment that winter with designs in geometric shapes: squares, diamonds and octagons against a flat ground. In *The Goblet* (page 72) the segments of the octagon are painted flatly, but upon them the drawing of a molding, a glass and a fragment of a cigarette package stands out as if in relief. These objects, particularly the glass with its superimposed rim, were a continuation of Braque's pre-war style; several of them —pipes, playing cards, guitars and bottles—were to reappear in his work of 1918-19, drawn with overlapping planes and multiple point of view.

Still Life with Grapes, 1918. Oil on canvas, 19 x 25". Collection Miss Marion G. Hendrie, Cincinnati

By the summer of 1918, after the lapse of the war years, Braque had recovered full control of his creative force. The continuity with his pre-war painting was not at first apparent except for the reappearance of the familiar still-life material; but now he began to represent volumes in space with some of the plastic quality and internal energy of his early cubist pictures. The colors became brighter and gayer, the forms larger and simpler.

Although Braque had begun to use color in 1914, his palette was still largely restricted to browns and blues. Picasso, however, was using very bright colors in certain pictures of 1914, such as the *Green Still Life* in the Museum of Modern Art. After the war, Braque accepted and assimilated this color scale, just as he did certain formal elements from Juan Gris.

His experiments in flat shapes produced the colorful *Still Life with Guitar* (page 81) in which wood grain reappears, and the almond-shaped *Still Life with Grapes* (above). The two-colored pattern of dots is taken from Picasso, but Braque handles it in his own manner; he fills his design with overlapping planes against which the insignia of the grape, the playing card and fragments of letters stand out with brilliance.

The most ambitious painting of these years is the huge *Musician* (page

75

Rum Bottle, 1918. Oil on canvas, 38¾ x 27½". Collection Mr. and Mrs. Joseph Pulitzer, Jr., St. Louis

The Buffet, 1919. Oil on canvas, 31⅞ x 39½". Private collection, Paris

78) completed, with some difficulty because of its size, in the attic studio of *Villa Bel Air* at Sorgues during the summer of 1918. The picture invites comparison with Picasso's Harlequin paintings to which it is certainly related. One could almost say that although the two men were no longer friends, their artistic collaboration continued. At least Braque continued to draw upon the creative force of the Spaniard. But as always, Braque recreates forms. No one but Braque could have conceived this huge vertical composition of overlapping planes which seem to float in and out of the picture space. Grained and dotted areas alternate with strips of flat color in a wonderful variety of decorative patterns. Long thin panels slope to one

The Musician, 1918. Oil on canvas, 90⅞ x 43½". Private collection, Paris

Café-Bar, 1919. *Oil on canvas,*
63¼ x 31⅞". Private collection, Paris

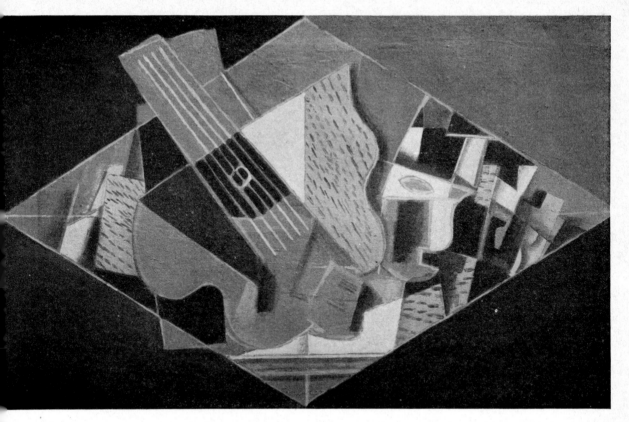

Still Life with Guitar, 1918-19. Oil on canvas, 23⅝ x 39⅜". Kröller-Müller Collection, Otterloo, The Netherlands

side and end in zigzags; the eye moves easily in and around the picture space until it is caught and held by the dark colors around the hands and guitar, the center of interest.

In the large oval still life of 1918, *Rum Bottle* (page 76), Braque engaged in a surprising renunciation of bright color. Most of the design is in white against a black ground, relieved only by areas of beige and brown. These are nearly the same colors as in the analytical paintings of 1911 and 1912, but with a rich black predominant instead of beige. However, the effect, if not as gay, is almost as decorative as the paintings in bright color. For instead of using the painted surface to define volume by means of angular planes, now Braque deals with pigment as a sensuous material, and all his skill as a trained apprentice comes into play. This skill had already appeared in his painting before the war, as briefly noted, and now he began to use it to enrich the surfaces of the large compositions of 1918. The areas of beige and brown are painted in thick pigment, and with loose brush strokes of a sort that had not been seen in French painting since Monet. The free curve meandering around rectilinear forms, that appeared once or twice in paint-

The Compote, 1919. Oil on canvas, 19¾ x 36¼". Private collection, Paris

ings of 1914, now reappears further to enhance the sensuous quality and to reduce the formal emphasis.

A variation of the theme and the color scheme is found in the *Still Life with Guitar*, 1919 (opposite), with a rich textural decoration of white and beige woven across the surface. The deep notes of black give the picture the greatest dignity and sobriety.

In the winter of 1918-19, Braque produced an exceptionally brilliant series of large still-life compositions. In the best of these he kept a balance between the geometric austerities of cubism on the one hand, and the vivid colors, richer surfaces and a growing relaxation of form which had appeared in his work since the war. The most impressive is a large vertical composition, the *Café-Bar* (page 79), one of the first to be composed around the little table known as a *guéridon*.[15] This was a round-topped, pedestal-based table that was in Braque's studio and it was to reappear with variations in his paintings for the next ten or twelve years. The table and large still-life group of tablecloth, tobacco, pipe, sheet music, newspaper, compote dish, grape, pear, guitar and guitar case are piled up vertically in a picture space which recedes because of a tiled floor at the base and gives room for the table's oak-brown legs. The objects hover against a background of polka-dotted red and green rectangular strips which here and there cross a panel of mahogany wood grain. In the upper background, one reads the huge letters CAFE—BAR as if they were on a shop window. The bright colors

82

Still Life with Guitar, 1919. Oil on canvas, 28¾ x 45¾". Collection Dr. E. Friedrich, Zurich

are quickly toned down by the surrounding ground of gray and black, in a contrast of gaiety and severity.

The Buffet (page 77) is a simpler treatment of the same theme but rectangular in shape, with similar objects and colors except for the introduction of two large panels in pale blue. The space is shallow and the planes seem to push out beyond the edges as if the composition could not contain them.

Another horizontal canvas of this year is *On the Table* (page 85). Its objects are severely flattened and surrounded by a double margin in angular patterns. In contrast to *The Buffet* its planes are held together by the table top and surrounded by a marginal space within the frame that does not cramp the composition.

In a vertical canvas (page 84), the *guéridon* is set in a dark background upon a tile floor with the central mass surrounded by curvilinear planes. Much of the color is brushed on loosely as in the *Café-Bar*. The letters JOURNAL turn and twist. The general design, although well composed, tends to be vague and shimmering. This same looseness of contours appears

83

Still Life on Table, 1918. Oil on canvas, 51¼ x 29⅛″. Private collection, Paris

On the Table, 1919. Oil and sand on canvas, 23 x 45". Collection Mr. and Mrs. Joseph Pulitzer, Jr., St. Louis

Life with Guitar and Letters RHUM, 1920. Oil on plaster. Present owner unknown

in a horizontal still life of 1919 (page 82). Now the brushwork is visible on much of the surface. The white guitar is shapeless and the compote dish lurches off to one side. It was perhaps of such a picture that Gris wrote: "I have seen some recent works of Braque which I find soft and lacking in precision. He is moving towards Impressionism."[16]

Léonce Rosenberg had been interested in cubism and had acquired a collection in his apartment on the rue Lavoisier. During the war he opened a gallery at 19 rue de la Baume, which he named *L'Effort Moderne*. He began to purchase and to show works by Picasso, Gris and other cubists at a time when they had almost no other market. Soon after Braque returned to his easel, Léonce Rosenberg bought some of his new paintings. In March, 1919 *L'Effort Moderne* held a Braque exhibition which gave the public its first opportunity since the war to see the painter's work.

This exhibition, coming a few months after the Armistice, in the midst of the early optimism of peace and the hoped-for revival of the arts, attracted a good deal of attention. Several of the articles in the press were favorable, particularly those of André Lhote and Bissière. The latter, a painter and friend of Braque's, had an extraordinary understanding of the

87

Still Life with Guitar and Letters POLKA, 1920. Oil on canvas. Collection Mr. and Mrs. Walter C. Arensberg, Hollywood

artist's style, which he described in an essay later published by *L'Effort Moderne*.[17] Braque now gained considerable fame and began to be looked upon as a leader of modern painting.

PERIOD OF TRANSITION

As already suggested, it is evident from the differing styles in his paintings of the year 1919 that Braque was struggling between the geometric discipline of cubism and a tendency towards sensuality which to Juan Gris appeared to be mere impressionism.

In 1920 he painted several still lifes in dark and somber tones, often with black as the predominating color, as in the *Still Life with Guitar and Letters* POLKA (above). The prevailing colors are black and white, green, brown and tan. A little later Braque used these colors and designs for vertical compositions too, as in the *Mantelpiece* of 1922 (opposite). Another type is the *Still Life with Guitar and Letters* RHUM of 1920 (page 87), painted on rough plaster so that it resembles stucco. In each of these paintings the letters have a bold, stencilled character, especially in the POLKA which perhaps has the effect of compensating for the softening contours. In spite of the boldness and strength of these paintings of the early twenties, there is a transitional element present, and it is found to a greater or lesser degree in all of the paintings of the period.

The Mantelpiece, 1922. Oil on canvas, 50 x 30". Collection Mr. and Mrs. Samuel A. Marx, Chicago

89

THE DEVELOPED STYLE (1920 TO DATE)

Still-Life is the specialty of Braque's genius. Seldom has painting touched with such enchantment things which in themselves appear of so little interest: fruit, flowers, loaves of bread, knives, jugs, packets of cigarettes and all our domestic accessories. Never were they so transfigured—unless it be by Chardin—by the magic of paint. Who but Braque, with animate brush and pigment, can so quicken their dormant life and open our eyes to their presence? He takes us into the kitchen, the bedroom, the dining room and the corners of his own studio in the pursuit of verity: nothing is too humble. Like Chardin before him, he dares display everything. But he has no recipe for beauty, no formula for composition; his work is free from stylisation and he returns time and again to the same subject with a determination to extract the last vestiges of its uniqueness.   There is nothing difficult or reprehensible in Braque's pictures, no riddles, no abstruse philosophical references, no hidden moral or meanings. One does not ask why the darker profile is imposed across the lighter full-face, nor why the billiard table appears "bent" in the middle. A painting by Braque has its own reality: it is not a copy of but a rival to nature. And so, from the lowliest objects Braque extracts a new poetry as he paints, and the outer world takes on for us a fuller, more exciting appearance. If we look, he will teach us to see, and this after all is the highest function of the true artist.[18]

DOUGLAS COOPER

The elements of Braque's new style are based on a return to natural appearances, but only a partial return. He retained many of the inventions and innovations of cubism and he never fell back on a mere copying of nature. This is what the painter himself has had to say on the matter:

One cannot achieve abstraction in speaking of abstraction. One's work would be like a blind alley. To arrive at abstraction one must start from nature, and to start from nature is to find a subject. If one loses contact with nature one will end fatally in decoration.

On the other hand those who begin by arranging still lifes and then try to paint them, are only imitating their own arrangements. For them painting becomes an act of doing *after* something, a lifeless imitation without feeling.

One can readily see his changed style in a red chalk drawing of 1920 (opposite). The pear is curved and rounded, quite true to natural appearance. The planes are shaded in chiaroscuro; the table and cover are drawn almost in perspective. Yet the guitar is vigorously stylized and the compote sliced down one side by an abrupt angular shadow. To realize the extent of the change in Braque's style, we may compare this work with a cubist drawing done in about 1912 (page 70).

At about this time Braque began to keep his drawings in notebooks and since then has accumulated several albums of them, which he keeps in his studio and uses for reference. The practice has probably contributed to the continuity of the motifs which run through all his work of the last twenty years. Even today he frequently turns to these piles of black bound books to make use of a head, a vase or some familiar pattern out of the past. Thus the compote invented in the drawing of 1920, reproduced below, will reappear with new context or color in paintings done five, ten and twenty years later.

In speaking of his style of drawing, Braque once remarked, "I have a heavy hand—which does not easily trace a contour. Whenever I begin doing a drawing, it turns into a painting—with hatching, shading and ornament."

About 1922, Braque began to use motifs of fruit in many of his still lifes. It was not a sudden innovation. The stylized bunch of grapes in a compote dish, although appearing but rarely in the pictures of 1912-14, became one of his favorite still-life elements from 1918 on. Now he added pears, apples and peaches to his repertory; later, lemons, oranges, plums and occasionally bananas or melons. In some of the small still-life paintings of 1922 (page 92), the drawing is sketchy and wavering but the paint is rich in variety of texture and color. The fruit is larger in proportion to the rest of the picture, and its surface gives a pretext for the most delicate ranges of color: the dark purple of a grape, the bloom of a peach, the yellow brown of a pear. These are the more delicate because of the low key of the surrounding colors:

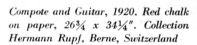

Compote and Guitar, 1920. Red chalk on paper, 26¾ x 34¼". Collection Hermann Rupf, Berne, Switzerland

91

Still Life with Fruit, 1920-22. Oil and sand on canvas, 13¾ x 29½″. Collection Arthur Bradley Campbell, Palm Beach, Florida

Figs and Grapes, 1922. Oil and sand on canvas, 7½ x 25½″. Private collection, New York

beige, gray, green and brown, subtly placed to interplay with contiguous
tones. The textures have the same harmonious interrelation: thin washes
contrasted with sandy areas, scratched wood grain or thick, irregular over-
paint. Often the fruit is arranged in a compote dish, sometimes with a
pitcher or other dish alongside, and placed upon a table against a background of wallpaper patterns. Parts of these pictures may be called impressionistic, or better, semi-impressionistic, but there is always a strong ele-

92

ment of cubism in Braque's treatment of volumes and space. He rarely gives the objects a feeling of sculptural roundness; more often he prefers to represent a low relief or even a flat surface. And the surrounding space is presented with shifting and overlapping planes very much as in the late cubist pictures of 1918-19. Because of the larger proportion of the fruit, the space seems to be closer to the spectator's eye, often closer than the normal angle of vision, so that one has the odd feeling of nearsightedness, as if one were expected to step up and look closely at an apple or a pear, and then move slightly to the right and inspect another detail of the picture.

NUDE FIGURES

Another phase of Braque's painting of the early twenties came out of his revived interest in the human figure. The small plaster sculpture of a female figure done in 1920 (below) seems to have been an attempt to reconcile the organic curves of the body with geometric or cubistic schematization. Not long after, he did a series of sketches and paintings which culminated in a pair of tall panels that Braque called *The Canephorae* or basket carriers.[19]

Figure, 1920. Plaster, 7¾" high. Buchholz Gallery, New York

Seated Nude, 1924. Black chalk on paper, 35½ x 28¾". Collection Dr. G. F. Reber and Frau Erna Reber, Chailly-sur-Lausanne, Vaud, Switzerland

These large semi-draped figures carrying baskets of fruit on their shoulders are inspired by classical subjects, as Braque made clear in his selection of the title. At the same time they are reminiscent of Renoir's vertical panels of gypsy dancers or Gauguin's Tahitian women. One also wonders to what extent Braque was attracted to this subject matter by Picasso's neo-classical figure painting which began in 1919.

Nevertheless, the Braque figures have a style entirely their own. The drawing of the torso is executed with the same wavering sketchy line found in the still lifes. The forms are ample, even Michelangelesque, the modeling broad and loose. The composition is remarkably well adapted to the vertical panels. The texture and pigmentation correspond to those in the paintings of fruit. The color is dark: skin tints are tan and purplish; the drapery is shot with contrasts of black and oyster white. These large nudes or semi-nudes have a neutral character and are quite devoid of sensual feeling. They seem to have been conceived with the same detachment and impassiveness one finds in a bowl of fruit or basket of flowers.

Nude with Basket of Fruit, 1924. Oil on canvas, 36 x 28". Collection Wright Ludington, Santa Barbara, California

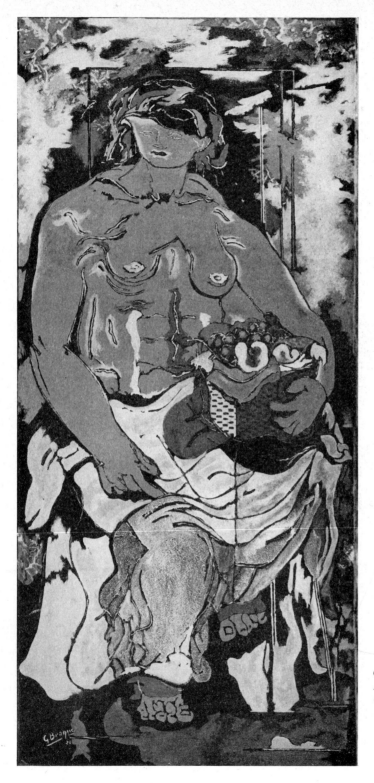

*Woman with Basket of Fruit, 1926.
Oil on canvas, 63½ x 29". Chester
Dale Collection. The Art Institute of
Chicago loan*

96

Nude, c.1924. Pencil and chalk on paper, 15 x 26". Collection Louis E. Stern, New York

After the first large pair of figure paintings, *The Canephorae*, Braque did several variations on this theme. Some were in the form of large drawings in charcoal, like the seated figure arranging her hair (page 94). Others were done as oil paintings. Occasionally the figure is reclining, but the most recurrent theme is a large semi-draped nude with flowing hair, holding a basket of fruit on either her lap or shoulder. The *Nude with Basket of Fruit*, 1924 (page 95), is painted in loose, flowing strokes, with the face partly in shadow so that it has a romantic and impassioned quality, like a figure by Delacroix. The colossal figure of 1926, in the Chester Dale Collection, sits impassively, without feeling, in a rich array of drapery against a marbleized background (opposite).

SUCCESS IN THE TWENTIES

In 1922 Braque was invited to exhibit a group of canvases at the *Salon d'Automne*. This was his first appearance in a *Salon* exhibition since the *Indépendants* show of 1909. He sent fourteen paintings including the large *guéridon* still lifes. The exhibition was a great success and all of his pictures were sold, one of them to Comte Etienne de Beaumont who later commissioned Braque to do a ballet set.

Since the success of Picasso's ballet decorations during the war, many of the younger painters had been commissioned to design sets and costumes. Braque went to Monte Carlo in the winter of 1923-24 to complete the décor of *Les Fâcheux* for the *Ballets Russes* of Serge Diaghilev.[20] The following

97

year he did the décor for *La Salade* which was ordered by the Comte de Beaumont for the *Soirées de Paris*, and also *Zephyr et Flore* for the *Ballets Russes*.

Kahnweiler returned to Paris about 1920 and soon opened the Galerie Simon at 29 bis rue d'Astorg. His pre-war picture stock had been sequestered by the French Government and was now ordered to be sold as alien property. These sales, which took place between 1921 and 1923, put large numbers of the finest cubist paintings by Braque, Picasso and Gris on the market at extremely low prices. Braque felt that Léonce Rosenberg, who had acted as an expert at the sales, might have been able to prevent this crash and the two men became estranged. In the meantime, Paul Rosenberg, Léonce's brother, who had recently begun to buy from Picasso, bought several of the Braques from his *Salon d'Automne* exhibition in 1922 and soon after that he signed a contract with Braque.

Braque held his first exhibition at the Rosenberg Gallery on the rue de la Boétie in May 1924, and from that date began to enjoy a commercial success. His prices, which with Léonce Rosenberg had been from eight hundred to one thousand francs, now advanced considerably, and he was able, like Picasso and Derain, to live in a manner quite different from that of the Bohemian days in Montmartre.

The Montmartre quarter had built up rapidly since the war and no longer preserved the semi-rural charm of the days of the *bateau-lavoir* and the *Lapin à Gill*. Picasso had moved to Montparnasse. Derain was living in Montsouris. In 1922 Braque's friend, the color merchant, Pierre Gaut, had taken him to the south side of Paris to look at the residential quarter around the Parc Montsouris and as a result Braque decided to build a house there on the Avenue Reill, near Ozenfant and not far from Derain. Braque lived in this house during 1923 and 1924. At that time he had met, through the painter Latapie, a young American architectural student named Paul Nelson. When Nelson learned that Braque was planning to build a larger house he persuaded him to engage the eminent architect, Auguste Perret, then Nelson's professor at the *Ecole des Beaux-Arts*. The design was worked out between Perret and Braque who had very definite ideas of what he wanted. This was the house at 6 rue du Douanier near Parc Montsouris, a three-story structure in brick and reinforced concrete, where Braque lives today. Its main feature is the large studio and study on the top floor, with a row of windows opening toward the south.

Derain owned a Bugatti racing car and not long after that, Braque bought an Alfa Romeo which he loved to drive at high speed. His friends agree that he was a very skillful driver, throwing himself into it with intensity and joy. There was a similar intensity in all of his recreation: bicycle rides, long walks, games of badminton. He is a fine gourmet and connoisseur and has always taken much pleasure in eating. Even the act of stopping his work to smoke a cigarette is something to be done with relish.

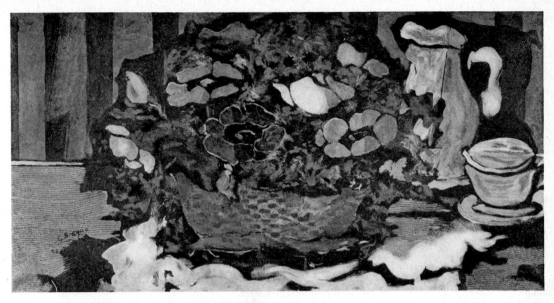

Anemones, 1925. Oil on canvas, 14¼ x 28¼". Private collection, New York

Mussels and Oysters, 1927. Oil and sand on canvas, 10¼ x 26⅞". Private collection, New York

NARROW RECTANGLES

Many of the canvases from the period beginning about 1921 are in the unconventional shape of a long narrow rectangle, with length from two to two and a half times its breadth. Just as Braque had revived the oval shape for the delightful contrasts it made with rectilinear cubist planes, now he devised this reduced surface to permit an intimate study of small objects without the need of composing structural elements to fill a large background. It was thus possible to paint two or three peaches, a plate, a napkin

99

Anemones, 1925. Oil and sand on canvas, 19½ x 24". Private collection, New York

and glass, to reveal the contrast of surfaces and colors and to bring out subtle harmonies. Some of Braque's most delightful pictures were made in these attenuated rectangular shapes.

The *Sugar Bowl with Fruit*, 1924, is a good example. Oranges, bananas and a lemon are placed beside a small porcelain sugar bowl and a glass that nearly touches the top of the canvas. Loosely brushed highlights move across the surfaces like sea foam, but in a dull-keyed, multi-colored harmony. As the French critic, Jean Grenier, wrote,

> Whoever does an essay on Braque should try to bring out how force-fully he uses the tactile space discovered by Cézanne, with what skill he manages to extract from the familiar, middle colors of the spectrum the most sumptuous harmonies, and finally how the matter of his painting seems as dense as the pulp of some fruit.[22]

A similar low-keyed and dense quality is found in the flower paintings of the twenties. In the last year or two Braque has painted many kinds of flowers but at that time he nearly always used anemones, probably because their variety of color and simple shape suited his pictorial needs. In the *Anemones*, 1925 (page 99), the flowers, foliage and basket are painted

100

The Mantelpiece, 1927. Oil on canvas, 51½ x 29¼". Norton Gallery and School of Art, West Palm Beach, Florida

Still Life, 1923. Oil on canvas, 25½ x 30″. Collection the Albright Art Gallery, Buffalo, New York. Room of Contemporary Art

in the closest harmony. Braque reduces the bright color of the flowers to dull pink and violet so that nothing will be out of place.

Another still-life motif of the twenties is the shellfish. Plates of shiny blue black mussels and oysters on the half-shell, with their cool translucent grays, reveal Braque's love for variations on the colors black and white (page 99). Often he would add a lemon or a napkin not only to enrich the play of color but perhaps also to evoke one's sense of taste, as Dutch still lifes do with their beakers of wine and plates of food. Braque might not readily concede this purpose in his painting, and certainly he aims at a higher level of appreciation. As he says: "I try to make an object lose its usual function. I only take it up after it is good for nothing else but the trash can, at the moment when its limitative use has ended. It is only then that it becomes the object of a work of art and acquires the quality of universality."

Black Rose, 1927. Oil on canvas, 20 x 37". Collection Mrs. Burton Tremaine, Jr., The Miller Company, Meriden, Connecticut

Guitar, Fruit and Pitcher, 1927. Oil and sand on canvas, 29 x 36″. Collection Mr. and Mrs. M. Lincoln Schuster, New York

SEVERE STYLE

At the same time that he did the narrow rectangles, Braque made a number of compositions on conventional shapes and also several vertical canvases which carry on the type he established in 1918-19. In these larger patterns the design is bolder, the treatment of detail less intimate. In the *Still Life*, 1923 (page 102), the objects are arranged on the edge of a mantelpiece as in certain paintings of 1922; the guitar, sheet music and pitcher are large in scale and their colors are dark and bold in contrast. The *Guitar, Fruit and Pitcher*, 1927 (above), is painted in severe, dark colors, but here they are relieved by planes of light blue. These canvases do not have the

105

Still Life with Grapes, 1927. Oil on canvas, 21 x 29". Collection The Phillips Gallery, Washington, D.C.

informality of the smaller pictures, but in the somber tones there is much dignity.

The vertical canvas, *The Mantelpiece*, 1927 (page 101) is also of this type. It is composed of large objects, dark colors and bold contrasts. The flat vertical panels, opposed by diagonals and curves, revives the mood of cubism. A severe but brightly colored picture of 1927 is the *Black Rose* (page 103), with its schematic divisions of light and shadow and the strongly emphasized floral pattern that Braque uses as a variation on the rose.

DECORATIVE STYLE

The *Still Life with Grapes*, 1927 (above) is a remarkable combination of qualities of intimacy and refinement with reminiscences of cubist design. Mr. Duncan Phillips has described the picture as follows:

The vignette of color shapes is a mass of rounded heavy contours, flat, straight-edged rectangles and inverted diagonals. Around this exciting

106

Still Life: The Table, 1928. Oil and sand on canvas, 32 x 53". Chester Dale Collection. The Art Institute of Chicago loan

center are quiet areas of opaque tones on unobtrusively tilted horizontals. The pattern can be analyzed as revealing a logical progression from the circles of the black spots on white cards and the green grapes in clusters to the ovals of the fruit bowls and the goblet and thence to the objects which curve only at the corners. The movement is vertical and circuitous, in and around the overlapping, radiating planes. They slip back in all but parallel recessions to a shallow space which is indicated by contours and directions, no longer by modulation of the planes. Each flat sheet seeks its place within the containing frame for the whole composition. Does this sound like a complicated organization? The reply from the eye is no. The effect is of life, crackling with expanding energy through a persuasive reason. The colors sing in vibrant chorus their unusual song of coal black and oyster white, or aristocratic intermediate tones, of pale blue, gunmetal gray, "café au lait," terra cotta, sand yellow and grape green.

During the next two years, 1928 and 1929, Braque painted a number of large still lifes, as bold in composition as those of 1927, but the colors of brown, dark green and black are now replaced by yellows, tans, blues and

107

The Table (Le guéridon), *1928. Oil on
canvas, 71 x 28¾". Collection Walter P.
Chrysler, Jr., Warrenton, Virginia*

The Table, 1928. Oil on canvas,
70¾ x 28¾". Collection the Museum of
Modern Art, New York. Acquired
through the Lillie P. Bliss Bequest

The Crystal Vase, 1929. Oil on canvas, 16 x 48¼". Private collection, New York

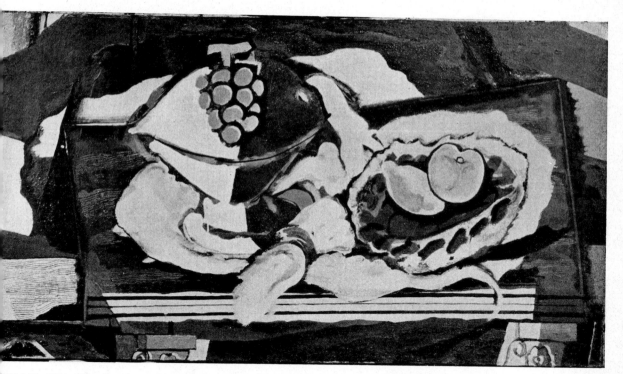

Still Life, 1928. Oil on canvas, 19¼ x 35½". Collection Mr. and Mrs. John Rood, Minneapolis

light greens, and patterns of ornamental wallpaper or wood grain appear more frequently. The loose brush strokes and impressionistic effects almost entirely disappear.

The *Still Life: The Table* of the Chester Dale Collection is a fine bold

111

The Round Table, 1929. Oil on canvas, 58 x 45″. Collection The Phillips Gallery, Washington, D. C.

ill Life: Le Jour, 1929. Oil on canvas, 45 x 57½". Chester Dale Collection. The Art Institute of Chicago

example; sand in the pigment gives the surface a texture like stucco (page 107). Another painting of 1928 is the *Still Life* (page 111). Here the dark colors and loose brushwork of the middle twenties are again used but with the addition of bright colors too.

Of these vertical compositions, perhaps the richest decorative painting of the year 1928 is *The Table* of the Museum of Modern Art (page 109). Like the late cubist *guéridon* paintings of 1919, the table is set on a tile floor which recedes gently to provide a commodious space. This is filled with a rich assortment of objects: guitar, tray, fruit, newspaper and fruit dish, shaped in free curves that tilt in thin vertical planes above the table and

113

move with delightful rhythm between the table top and the tall double-panelled screen. The entire surface is enriched in a rough sandy grain that restrains the gaiety and yet is pleasant to touch—another of those subtle combinations of sensuality and sobriety so typical of Braque.

A handsome variation on this composition, executed at the same time, is *The Table* of the Chrysler Collection (page 108). Here the objects are grouped on a square-topped, knobby-legged table, with less compactness, but with a charming line that wanders around the mandolin, zigzagging over the sheet music, winding again around the compote dish, and moves in a quick diagonal across the pipe coming to rest on the round door handle. The two panels seen side by side provide an extraordinary glimpse at the artist's method of variation on a theme.

Another equally rewarding comparison can be made between two large horizontal still lifes done in 1929: *The Round Table* of The Phillips Gallery (page 112) and the *Still Life: Le Jour* of the Chester Dale Loan at the Art Institute of Chicago (page 113). In both canvases the bisected guitar protrudes sharply on the left side while a hunting knife lies in the foreground. As in the vertical pictures, the round *guéridon* may be contrasted with the square oak table. Braque has composed both pictures with a sense of self-confidence and boldness that is rare in his work. One is tempted to compare them with the large still lifes that Picasso had been painting in 1924-26, and which were also being exhibited at the Paul Rosenberg Gallery. If there was a spirit of competition or jealousy between the two men, Braque is reluctant to admit it today.

In these same years Braque painted several canvases in the long thin rectangular format last used in the early twenties. Most of these were larger: from three to four feet long. With the special compositional conditions they provide, these panels do not make the bold demands on space or color that have just been noted in the large pictures of these years. Braque continued to use his subtler effects, the neutral tones, the blacks and dark green marbleized surfaces. The panels almost speak a different language than the large pictures. *The Crystal Vase* (page 111) was once part of a group of four that decorated the Paris dining room of Paul Rosenberg, and their designs were repeated in mosaics on the floor.

To anyone familiar with French interiors, these tall vertical shapes and long narrow rectangles will be reminiscent of the gracefully carved *chutes d'armes* and painted *dessus de portes* of the Louis XV style. The designs of Braque's panels lend themselves perfectly to the tapestries that Madame Cuttoli has had woven from them. But in spite of their suavity and good taste, and predominantly decorative appeal, the paintings are redeemed by qualities more vital to the work of art, by the tension of subtle inner relationships of the objects as they exist in space and by the constant or varying evocations of reality.

114

Cliffs and Fishing Boat, 1929. Oil on canvas, 13 x 18". Private collection, New York

VARENGEVILLE

Every summer since the war Braque and his wife had returned to the *Villa Bel Air* at Sorgues. Occasionally they made short visits to other parts of the *Midi*, and in 1925, after a fortnight at La Ciotat with the Pierre Gauts, they talked of buying a house on the *Côte d'Azur*, but Madame Braque felt that her husband would never be happy for long in the south. As Derain, who was also there, remarked, the light on the Mediterranean shore is too bright for a painter. It makes everything look black and white.

The Paul Nelsons spent their summers in upper Normandy near Dieppe and one year they invited the Braques. Braque was delighted with the rolling countryside, the fertile meadows and valleys, the gorse on the hills near the Channel. The chalk cliffs, with their vast white surfaces, gave the light a soft diffused quality that constantly changed under the shifting clouds. The

115

The Table (Le guéridon), 1930. Oil on
canvas, 57⅝ x 30⅜". Collection Mr.
and Mrs. Jacques Helft, Buenos Aires

116

The Blue Mandolin, 1930. Oil on canvas, 46¼ x 34⅝″. Collection City Art Museum of St. Louis

Normandy landscape, the local dialect, the thatched cottages and the sea all reminded Braque of his youth at Le Havre.

In the summer of 1929 the Braques rented a house at Dieppe and soon after that bought some land at Varengeville about five miles south and just

117

out of sight of the coast. Here he put up a Norman cottage from Paul Nelson's designs. Nelson had tried in vain to design a modern villa with flat roof and glass walls. Braque wanted the seclusion of walls with small windows, and he thought that the roof and exterior should follow the Norman traditions (below). The house was completed early in 1931, the studio a little later. Since that date Braque has made many long sojourns at Varengeville, usually staying late into the autumn.

After coming to Varengeville, Braque began to paint landscapes again for the first time since La Roche-Guyon. The earliest of these were some views of the harbor at Dieppe, but the subject he painted most often was the pebbly beach. He developed a composition with fishing boats, small sheds and overhanging cliffs, using rich and varied colors (page 115). The pebbles behind the fishing boat "D 27" are dark and luminous, like precious stones. The *Beach at Dieppe* belonging to the Museum of Modern Art is colored black, blue, gray and yellow. If these colors seem arbitrary, they are nevertheless suggested by the ever changing tints on the beach which run from dark gray and black to pale blue and lavender. Most of these landscape canvases were quite small. One reason for this was the difficulty of moving back and forth from Paris. Braque used to start packing three or four days before departure and the huge canvases he kept in the studio were impossibly cumbersome on the roof of his small car.

In 1930 Braque painted several large colorful still-life compositions similar to those done in the previous two years. Of these, the *Guitar and Bottle of Marc* (color frontispiece) is one of the strongest. The bisected guitar is again the main motif, but now it is presented in a variation upon the colors of red and blue. The surfaces of tablecloth, rug, woodwork, wallpaper, dado

The artist's home at Varengeville

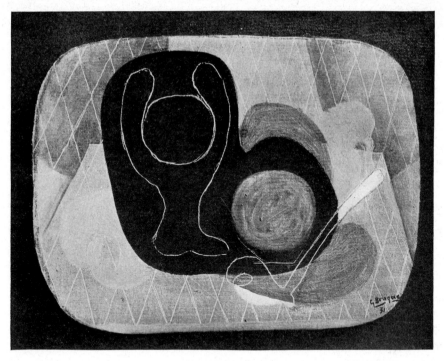

The Clay Pipe, 1931. Oil on canvas, 10¾ x 13¾". Collection the Museum of Modern Art, New York

and wainscoting are represented in overlapping planes opposing verticals to horizontals, plain surfaces to ornamented, lights to shadows, warm colors to cool in a rich variety. That all this wealth of detail can be discovered in a painting which at first glance appears to be bold and simple, is further evidence of Braque's extraordinary capacity for assimilating divergent plastic elements into a harmonious whole. Variations on this theme are *The Blue Mandolin* (page 117), of the City Art Museum of St. Louis and the *guéridon* in terra-cotta red with long sweeping curves that fill the composition with a new kind of rhythm (page 116).

CANVASES WITH THIN PAINT

Toward the end of the year 1930, Braque began to paint in a manner quite unlike anything he had done before. The long sweeping curves noticed in the Helft picture now begin to dominate the design at the expense of other details. Overlapping planes, ornaments, textures, rich combinations of color all tend to disappear. The drawing traces flat shapes with curvilinear outlines, the oil pigment is diluted and applied in thin washes like water color. Whatever the reasons for the abrupt change of style, many admirers of

119

Apples, 1933. Oil on canvas, 35 x 45¾". Collection Walter P. Chrysler, Jr., Warrenton, Virginia

Braque's painting judge this period harshly. Others profess to find in it delicate qualities of line and transparent color. One might guess that Braque had become apprehensive of the increasing decorative quality in his large canvases of 1928-30 and now determined to purify his style in a radical manner. This seems a plausible explanation, since he had submitted to a similar self-discipline in dropping the *fauve* style, and again in 1919-20 with the still lifes in dark colors.

During 1931 Braque painted several large still-life compositions in this manner, with thin washes of tan, black and rose. The small *Clay Pipe* 1931, of the Museum of Modern Art, is a characteristic work of this period. The contour lines are a reversal of the usual drawing technique. They are scratched in the paint down to the bare canvas leaving a kind of wiry vacuum around the objects (page 119).

A striking exception to the paintings of this year is *The Red Tablecloth* (page 122). The pigment is thin as in the other canvases but the color is gay and the design is based on the rich ornamentation of the 1930 still lifes.

Possibly inspired by beach scenes at Varengeville, Braque painted a number of bathing groups in 1931 (opposite) but they were drawn in a manner radically different from the buxom nudes of the early twenties. The

Apples, 1934. Red chalk on paper, 19½ x 26½″. Collection Richard S. Davis, Wayzata, Minnesota

The Bathers, 1931. Oil on canvas, 51½ x 77″. Collection Walter P. Chrysler, Jr., Warrenton, Virginia

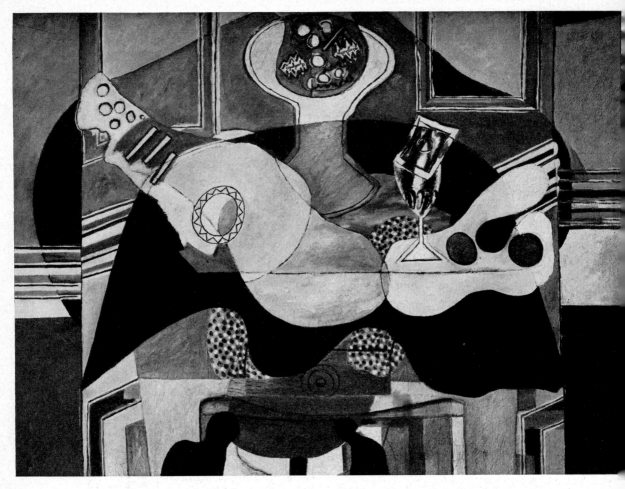

The Red Tablecloth, 1931. Oil on canvas, 34¾ x 45¼". Collection Mrs. Edna K. Warner, Fort Lauderdale, Florida

colors are pale gray, pink and blue and the line seeks a flowing arabesque. The very free treatment of the figures, the grotesque distortions and the preoccupation with sex are without precedent in Braque's previous work. To find an explanation for the sudden appearance of these foreign elements in Braque's painting, one must conclude that he had been impressed by certain Picasso figure paintings of 1928-30.

NEO-CLASSICISM

In 1930-31 Braque again became interested in ancient Greek art and made a number of sketches of nymphs and heroes. These were drawn in a thin sensuous line that imitates the late archaic style. Often he introduced

122

curious fantasies: figures with crescent heads or snowshoe feet and inscriptions in Greek letters.

His source appears to have been Greek vase painting, and possibly Etruscan mirrors, both of which are well represented in the Louvre Museum. He also had consulted the illustrations in books on ancient art, and must have been familiar with the line engravings in eighteenth-century books— particularly those dealing with engraved stones (abraxas).[22]

While working with this material Braque developed a new medium. The ground was a plaster plaque, which he painted in black and then engraved. This seemed better suited to the archaic subject matter than pencil drawings or oil sketches, and some of his finest neo-classic designs were done in these *platres gravés* (below).

Ambroise Vollard, who had published a number of de luxe editions of illustrated books, such as Ovid's *Metamorphoses* with Picasso's illustrations, now commissioned Braque to illustrate Hesiod's *Theogony*. The artist made sixteen etchings, working in the same manner of free linear arabesques (page 156).

Braque also did a few large-scale canvases in the neo-classic style, especially a group of wall panels in 1932 for the Paris apartment of a Monsieur Holzschuch.[23]

Herakles, 1932. Engraved plaster. Sacher Collection, Basel, Switzerland

Since 1925 Braque had been represented in numerous exhibitions in Paris and other European cities, but the largest exhibition of his career up to that time was held at the Kunstmuseum of Basel in April, 1933. It was arranged by the Swiss collector, Frau Sacher-Hoffman, and was an event of international importance like the large Matisse show held in Zurich the year before.

1933 marks the end of Braque's thin period. That year he began a series of still-life compositions with pink as the predominating color, enriched with a variety of texture and ornament quite as decorative as any of the 1928-30 paintings. *The Pink Tablecloth* (opposite) has some of the same motifs found

The Yellow Tablecloth, 1935. Oil on canvas, 45 x 57". Collection Mr. and Mrs. Samuel A. Marx, Chicago

The Pink Tablecloth, 1933. Oil and sand on canvas, 38⅛ x 51¼". Collection Walter P. Chrysler, Jr., Warrenton, Virginia

The Cliffs, 1938. Oil on canvas, 19¾ x 25¾". Collection Mr. and Mrs. Leigh B. Block, Chicago

in the *Apples* (page 120), especially the pear-shaped carafe on the left side, but the flowing arabesque is now strung in loops, the tablecloth ends in a toothy zigzag, the entire painted surface is finished with a sandy texture, and above all, as the title suggests, it is in the gayest bright pink color.

Another phase of Braque's style in the mid-thirties can be seen in *The Yellow Tablecloth*, 1935 (page 124). This picture was the first-prize winner at the Carnegie Exhibition of 1937 and again two years later at the Golden Gate Exhibition in San Francisco. It is a still-life composition not unlike the large *Le Jour* of 1929, but the spectator's eye level is imagined to be at a point below the table top, so that the objects are silhouetted against the cornice and ceiling. The color key is taken from the yellow tablecloth but every part of the canvas is so pale that there is an unusually delicate suggestion of objects in a spacious room.

DOUBLE-IMAGE FIGURES

In many of the still lifes of the twenties, Braque represented certain still-life elements in an arbitrary black-and-white division of light and shade, especially the pitcher or the guitar. In the late thirties he began to

127

Painter and Model, 1939. Oil on canvas, 51 x 69". Collection Walter P. Chrysler, Jr., Warrenton, Virginia

use this device in designing the human figure. When a plane representing another point of view is overlapped on a pitcher it usually remains a part of the same pitcher or glass or compote dish. But when one sees this device on the face and torso with long angular planes repeating the contours of organic shapes—one side dark, one light—the image tends to become two figures or perhaps a substance and a shadow, and a new ray of psychological meaning enters the picture. This is what happened in the figure paintings begun in 1936, a series depicting a woman painter seated before her easel. Strange angular Siamese twins vacillate uneasily between black profile and pale torso. The floating, overlapping planes seen in Braque's earlier pictures are here kept in the background, and the surrounding room space is furnished with the artist's studio possessions, as if he himself were somewhere in the distance. The *Woman with a Mandolin*, 1937, is a variation on this

128

Woman with a Mandolin, 1937. *Oil on canvas,* 51¼ x 38¼". *Collection the Museum of Modern Art, New York. Mrs. Simon Guggenheim Fund*

The Studio, 1939. Oil on canvas, 45 x 57½". Collection Paul Rosenberg, New York

theme (page 129). Tall and graceful as an El Greco saint, she sits like an ambiguous shadow in this tensely colored room.

Another painting in the figure series is the large *Painter and Model*, 1939 (page 128), in which the blacks and yellow greens are woven into a tapestry-like design. Here a second figure steps into the picture, a thin unfamiliar fellow with a goatee and a cigar.

In two or three still lifes of this year, Braque used the skull as a motif, and this object has since reappeared in a half-dozen paintings, the latest of them completed in 1943. Often the skull is accompanied by a cross or rosary. It has been said that Madame Braque, who is very devout, aroused Braque's interest in the religious overtones of the subject, but the artist has not acknowledged this as the source of his inspiration.

131

Pitcher, Bread and Lemon, 1939. Oil on canvas, 18 x 22". Collection Mr. and Mrs. Leigh B. Block, Chicago

SCULPTURE

While at Varengeville in the summer of 1939, Braque made some carvings in local chalkstone but the material was so soft that he cast it in plaster. This was the beginning of his recent work in sculpture. *The Pony* (page 134), which was later cast in bronze, dates from that year.

As his friend Henri Laurens put it, a painter becomes curious about how his painted forms look on the other side and makes sculpture of them in order to find out. The remark is appropriate to Braque because in general he has designed his sculpture in only two planes: front and back, although *The Pony* is an exception.

Upon returning to Paris, Braque built a sculpture studio near his home and spent much of his time there during the winter of 1939-40. He made a

Head of a Horse, 1946? Bronze, 38½" long. Buchholz Gallery, New York

bronze urn which is in his home, and several profile heads. In 1942 he did the *Fish* (below) and several years later, the large *Head of a Horse* (above), which seems to have been inspired by the marble head from the Parthenon in the British Museum. In spite of the war, Braque managed to obtain metal and the head was cast in three or four copies: two in lead, one in yellow bronze and another in dark bronze. Braque also experimented with curious objects in plaster, like the bottom of a bowl or a broken plaque. These he painted with designs of black and terra cotta so that they looked like fragments of primitive pottery (page 136). Some of the plaster plaques he carved in relief and left white, such as the *Io* (page 135). Others were painted with a bright blue background, as the *Uranie* of the Galerie Maeght.

Fish, 1942. Bronze, 14" long. Buchholz Gallery, New York

133

The Pony, 1939. Bronze, 7¼″ high. Collection Wright Ludington, Santa Barbara, California

THE OCCUPATION

In the spring of 1940 when the German armies broke through the Maginot Line, Braque was at Varengeville. He and his wife and their maid, Mariette Lachaud, gathered together their possessions including all of the recent paintings and managed to drive south to the house of Mariette's parents, in the province of Limousin. There they found a place to hide the paintings and after remaining a month, they went on further south to Ariège in the Pyrenees and after that to Castillon. Finally in the autumn they made their way back to the Paris house, where Braque remained throughout the war.

The house across the street was occupied by German officers and Braque knew that if he moved from his own house it would be taken over immediately. He was never molested, even though he refused invitations to travel in Germany and exhibit his paintings there—invitations which some of his former friends accepted. He also turned down a request to design an emblem for the Vichy Government.

During the frightful year of 1940, Braque did very little painting, but in 1941 he began to work again both in sculpture and oil painting. Canvas and colors were as difficult to obtain as food, but there were friends who managed to help.

The Rosenberg Gallery had been closed since 1939. Braque sold some of

134

his paintings at the gallery of Louise Léiris, the wife of the poet Michel Léiris, and sister-in-law of Kahnweiler, who was hiding in the South. After 1943 he began to sell paintings through the Galerie Maeght which had opened in Paris during the occupation.

NEW SUBJECT MATTER

By 1942 Braque's paintings had again developed a vigorous and fertile style and his studio was filled with large canvases. Often he applied the paint loosely and in large surfaces, almost as if he were painting hurriedly. Consequently some of the pictures of that year and the next have a rather sketchy quality, very different from the intricate organization of the work he had been doing in the late thirties.

A motif for several paintings of 1942 is a large blue pitcher, which he arranged with a wash bowl and toilet articles on a table by a window. As in the pre-war figure paintings, Braque composed these objects in a room space which established a different kind of relationship between the objects and their surroundings (page 138). Instead of the internal dynamism of his cubist still lifes, in which the objects lose part of their identity and become semi-abstract symbols, these are composed with more naturalism. They invite us to enter the room space, to identify the objects in relation to their function. Often they invoke a mood of romanticism. In one of the variations a woman turns her bare back and looks at the clouds outside the window.

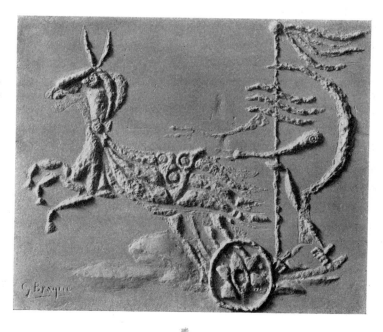

Io, 1939. Plaster relief, 8⅝ x 10¾".
Collection Dr. and Mrs. F. R.
Hensel, Indianapolis

135

Broken Bowl, 1940? Plaster, 6" diameter. Owned by the artist

In another the French windows open on a stormy sky, and the objects within: pitcher, sponge and tablecloth are agitated in form (page 139). The shame and tragedy of defeated France had obviously found their way into Braque's heart.

Another motif of the war years is the kitchen still life. In place of the symbols of Bohemianism, café life, or luxury, Braque now turned to a repertory of household objects: coffee grinder, frying pan, a loaf of bread, a pair of fish. These homely objects in certain still lifes of the mid-forties have a dignity and simplicity quite unlike the moody atmosphere of the blue wash basins. One of the finest is a vertical composition: *Kitchen Still Life*, 1942 (page 140), whose content and style are close to Chardin. A variation on the homely theme is *The Stove*, 1944 (page 147). This is painted with the broad brushstrokes of the blue pictures of 1942, but with rich new combinations of texture and ornament and less stress upon mood.

The large *Salon* of 1944, belonging to the Musée National d'Art Moderne in Paris, is perhaps the most successful painting of interior space completed during these years (page 143). It marks a return to the expression of luxury and optimism. There is an air of serenity in this black table placed so harmoniously in its cool surroundings.

After a lapse of several years, Braque again began to paint flowers. The *Flowers on Box*, 1942, is composed with a combination of deep brown, lavender, pink and blue, which Braque has woven into a unified color scheme by rich variations of pigment and brushstroke (page 142). Other flower paintings were made in 1946, including a series of sunflowers (page 151) and the bright green and gold still life (page 150).

Interior, 1942. Oil on canvas, 57 x 77". Hugo Art Gallery, New York

LIBERATION

Braque's first Paris exhibition after the liberation was a triumph, and soon after that the whole world began to hear of his recent paintings. The next year he was made an officer of the Legion of Honor. After V-E Day his wartime paintings went on a tour of the European capitals: Brussels, Amsterdam and later to London, where Braque attended the opening.

Braque's formerly robust health suffered during the privations of the war and in 1945 he underwent a stomach operation. For several months he was unable to return to his painting. Early in 1946 he was back at work in his studio, completing the group of canvases which had been left unfinished at the time of the operation.

137

The Blue Wash Basin, 1942. Oil on canvas, 23½ x 31½". Collection Mr. and Mrs. Abner Goldstone, New York

The house at Varengeville was not far from the beaches at Dieppe which had been the scenes of the ill-fated landing operations of 1942. Braque, who had been at Dieppe at the time, was apprehensive about the state of his house but on returning in September 1944, found it intact. It had been occupied by German troops who had damaged the one painting left behind, a small still life. Since the liberation, the Braques have returned frequently to Varengeville. The movie short made by *Actualités Françaises* in 1945 shows him there walking in the cemetery of the little church nearby. In the spring of 1947, walking along the cliffs, Braque caught a cold that developed into pneumonia. His friend, the young painter De Stael, managed to get him into the American hospital at Neuilly, where under the care of Dr. Soullard, he was treated with penicillin and cured. Today, although he has lost some of his former vigor, he still paints every morning.

Washstand at Window, 1942. Oil on canvas. Owned by the artist

139

Kitchen Still Life, 1942. Oil on canvas, 65⅛ x 31½". Collection Jean Paulhan, Paris

Still Life with Fish, 1942. Oil on canvas. Collection the Musée National d'Art Moderne, Paris

Since the liberation Braque has made several color lithographs (page 159) both of still lifes and neo-classic subjects (printed by Mourlot Frères). The subjects of most of these were first developed in oil paintings: still life with a teapot, a charioteer. But as is often the case in such transpositions, the subjects are so well adapted to the new medium that some prefer the lithographs to the oil paintings. The charioteer motifs are, like his earlier neo-classic work, adaptations from archaic Greek and in all probability they are free interpretations of engraved stones (abraxas). This would account not only for the chariot and the inscriptions but also for the oval shapes.

LATEST PAINTINGS

The subjects of his most recent paintings are flowers, garden chairs and billiard tables. In an arbor beside the front of his house are two or three metal chairs which recently caught the artist's eye as subjects for painting. In drawings the chair-back becomes an arabesque. In the painting its green

141

Flowers on Box, 1942. Oil on canvas, 34 x 24". Collection Mr. and Mrs. Leo Glass, New York

The Salon, 1944. Oil on canvas, 47⅜ x 58¾". Collection the Musée National d'Art Moderne, Paris

color is placed against a light ground, and enriched with textures and variations that have been built up by weeks of work (pages 152 and 153).

One of *The Billiard Table* received the first prize for foreign painting last summer at the Biennial Exhibition in Venice (page 149). A larger and richer variation (page 155) is now in progress and Braque has been working on it through the summer and late fall of 1948, slowly adding to the rich yellow green surface.

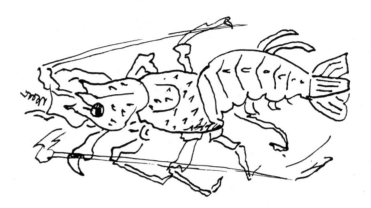

BRAQUE'S THEORIES ON ART

In recent years Braque has prepared a series of lithographs illustrating aphorisms and thoughts that he had been gathering in his notebooks for thirty years. These were published in a portfolio entitled *Cahier de Georges Braque.* From these aphorisms and other recent statements one can learn something of the aims and theories of the artist.

Perhaps the most recurrent idea is found in the series of statements relating to his theory of art and nature.

> One should not imitate what one wishes to create.
>
> I would much rather put myself in unison with nature than copy it.
>
> Nature does not give the taste for perfection. One conceives of it as neither better nor worse.
>
> To define something is to substitute the definition for the thing.
>
> Some artists paint nature as a taxidermist stuffs an animal, believing that they are thus making her immortal.

Art for Braque is certainly not the imitation of nature. Yet he has been quoted earlier in the text (page 90) as saying that "one must start from nature." If he is not clear on the next step, we can perhaps grasp a part of his meaning from such statements as:

> The painter thinks in forms and colors, the object is his poetic aim.
>
> The painter knows things from sight, the writer by name.

145

The Green Tablecloth, 1943. Oil on canvas, 18⅛ x 24¾". Collection the Musée National d'Art Moderne, Paris

In art there is only one thing of value, that which cannot be explained [i.e. explained in words].

The painter does not attempt to restate an anecdote but to get at the essence of a pictorial fact.

Form and color do not mix, they are simultaneous.

A lemon and orange side by side cease to be a lemon and an orange and become fruits. The mathematicians follow this law; so do we.

To those who have criticized Braque for being only a painter of still lifes, he would give this answer: "Limited means engender new forms, invite creation and produce a style," or "Progress in art does not consist in extending one's limitations, but in knowing them better."

A recent visitor to his studio was astonished to find it filled with plants and bouquets of flowers, carefully arranged on tables around the room, crowding against bottles and jars, tubes and brushes but as meticulous and orderly as a still-life painting. Upon finding several unfinished flower com-

The Stove, 1944. Oil on canvas, 57⅝ x 35″. Galerie Maeght, Paris

147

Woman at a Mirror, 1946. Oil on canvas. Collection Valentine Dudensing, Paris

The Billiard Table, 1945. Oil on canvas. The Musée National d'Art Moderne, Paris

positions on the easels, the visitor asked if these bouquets were used as models. Braque replied that he did not paint directly from the object [as he had done when a student], that the flowers on his canvas were drawn from many bouquets he had seen and remembered, that his memory was rich with images that he wished to paint, that that was one advantage of being old. As he put it in another way in the last aphorism of his book, "With age art and life become one."

The above paragraph gives only a hint of the mystery of the artist's process of creation but he was a little more revealing in a conversation of a few years ago,

Impregnation is that which comes to us unconsciously, which is developed and retained by obsession and which is delivered up one day by creative hallucination.

Hallucination is the definitive realization of a long impregnation whose beginnings may go back to youth.

149

Still Life with Flowers, 1946. Oil on canvas, 34¾ x 43". Collection Stephen C. Clark, New York

The age of impregnation is early youth. I find that I am painting today the most anonymous aspirations of my beginning, things that touched me at the time without my being aware of it and which have since pursued me until this final realization.[26]

As to his method of composing, of planning the picture he is about to paint, Braque insists on the elements of intuition and mystery as a part of the creative process. "I discover my picture on the canvas the way a fortune teller reads the future in tea leaves."

Braque was even more specific in a recent interview:

I could not do otherwise than I do. The picture makes itself under the brush. I insist on this point. There must be no preconceived idea. A picture is an adventure each time. When I tackle the white canvas I

150

The Sunflowers, 1946. Oil on canvas, 41¼ x 41¼". Collection The Reader's Digest, Pleasantville, New York

never know how it will come out. This is the risk you must take. I never visualize a picture in my mind before starting to paint. On the contrary I believe that a picture is finished only after one has completely effaced the idea that was there at the start.[27]

151

The Chair, 1946. Charcoal on paper, 18½ x 24″. Collection David Mann, New York

BRAQUE'S METHOD OF PAINTING

Braque works on several paintings at a time, often keeping as many as thirty unfinished canvases in his studio. There are usually five or six on easels where he can study them, but when painting he places the canvas on the easel nearest the light. He may work on one for a few hours, or for several days and then move it to a distant easel for drying. In the summer of 1948, the largest canvas in the studio was *The Billiard Table* mentioned before, which is nearly six feet wide. There were two or three flower compositions and a large study of a green chair.

One morning he started a new painting of the garden chair. He traced the pattern of the chair from the other painting and transposed it to the new canvas. To this he added a second chair in a free variation and then began to apply color. By the end of the day Braque had sketched in the broad outlines of these chairs in yellow green, filling the white areas around them with light blue. Across the top he added a broad strip of black. The surface of the canvas was about half covered with pigment. Here and there were color notes written in for later use. The canvas was later stood on the floor where it remained for about a week and it was probably several weeks

152

The Chair, 1947. Oil on canvas, 25⅝ x 19″. Galerie Maeght, Paris

before Braque got around to painting on it again. Some of his paintings remain in the studio for six months or a year before he considers them finished.

Oddly enough when Braque finally considers a painting finished he loses interest in it. He has none of that possessive quality attributed to Degas. Very few of his paintings hang in his house and they are not always the best. As he declared in a conversation with a journalist,

> When a picture leaves my house it is for always. When I see one in a collection I sometimes even have the impression that it is not by me. I

never repaint earlier pictures. If I had the desire to do so it would become another painting.

When asked what effect the sand mixed in his pigment might have upon the color, he replied that far from harming it, the sand seemed to give greater permanence. His studio is filled with equipment, several easels and palettes and dozens of jars and tubes of paint. Braque handles his brush with a masterly skill, and it is something like watching a virtuoso violinist to see him apply paint. Yet Braque is never a virtuoso; he is something far rarer—a master craftsman.

HENRY R. HOPE
INDIANA UNIVERSITY

Photographs of the artist and his studio, June, 1948. Photo Fritz Henle

PRINTS AND ILLUSTRATIONS

In 1912 Daniel Henry Kahnweiler, dealer and early propagandist of cubism, published Braque's first prints, the two drypoints *Fox* and *Job*. *Fox*, perhaps Braque's most important print in any medium, was the name of a Paris bar near St. Lazare where Apollinaire and his friends occasionally gathered. *Job* refers to the brand name of a popular cigarette tobacco. Kahnweiler, who also issued Picasso's cubist prints, continued to publish most of Braque's graphic work.

Ten years later in 1922, and again in 1933, Braque experimented briefly with color lithography, but not until 1944 did he seriously explore the medium. Working with the master lithographer Fernand Mourlot, he used four to six stones for as many colors in a single print. As variations on a theme the most interesting of these lithographs are the *Helios* series begun in 1946. The central design, Helios in his chariot, is identical in all six ver-

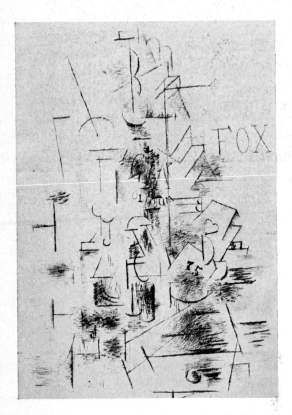

Fox, 1912. Drypoint, 21½ x 15". Collection the Museum of Modern Art, New York

Goddess on Horseback, c.1932. Etching, 14½ x 11¾". Collectio[n] the Museum of Modern Art, New York

156

Helios (IV), 1947. Color lithograph, 20 x 16¾". Collection James William Reid, N. Y.

Helios (I), 1946. Lithograph, trial proof, 10⅝ x 9⅛". Collection the Museum of Modern Art, New York. Gift of Victor S. Riesenfeld

sions and was printed from the same stone. The colors and background of each version vary, however, and were made from different stones.

Including several lithographs which exist only in trial proof, Braque's graphic work totals forty-five individual prints, two thirds of which were intended as book illustrations. His first woodcuts were cut in 1921 to decorate Erik Satie's *Le Piège de Méduse*. Ten years later Ambroise Vollard commissioned illustrations to Hesiod's *Theogony*. Braque began preliminary drawings in 1931, but the book remained unpublished at the time of Vollard's death in 1939. An edition of the sixteen etchings without text, however, had been made. To Einstein's monograph on Braque, published in 1934, the artist contributed two etchings. For more recent de luxe editions by his friends and critics he has designed color lithographs as covers, frontispieces and page decorations. The special edition of his own facsimile *Cahier de Georges Braque* contains two lithographs, one in color repeating the Helios motif, the other in black and white.

Although Braque's prints are individual to his work as a painter, he has tried most graphic media. During the early thirties he engraved many designs on plaster. These, like many of his prints, refer to Greek legends but the plasters themselves were neither intended nor used as plates from which to print. They are incised drawings, each unique, and not part of his oeuvre as a print maker.

WILLIAM S. LIEBERMAN

Io, 1945. Color lithograph, 12⅛ x 17". Collection the Museum of Modern Art, New York. Acquired through the Lillie P. Bliss Bequest

Opposite:

Teapot and Lemon, 1947. Color lithograph, 14⅜ x 21¾". The Buchholz Gallery, New York

158

NOTES TO THE TEXT

1. The artist is not certain of this date. 2. One of these, a small marine subject of 1899, is owned by the French writer, Jean Paulhan. 3. From a communication by R. Pissarro to John Rewald. 4. See Robert Goldwater, *Primitivism in Modern Painting*, New York, Harper, 1938. 5. Braque thinks this may have been said in 1904, in which case he would have been at Honfleur in 1905. 6. Fernande Olivier, *Picasso et ses amis*, Paris, Stock, 1933, p. 120. 7. *The New York Times* art page of Oct. 8, 1911, in a report on cubist paintings which its correspondent (Gelett Burgess) had seen in Paris, said: *There is Georges Braque who paints nudes with square feet and right-angled shoulders. Before one of his weird productions, a woman with a balloon-shaped stomach, we remarked "a wild place fit for dreams but no place for mother."* This painting was one of three by Braque in the Armory Show of 1913, where it was entitled *The Violin*. *Musical America* of March 22, 1913 commented as follows: *If the beholder can find any resemblance to a violin in Mr. Braque's painting, so we are assured, it is not because the artist set out to reproduce the instrument but because the vividness of the impression made the fiddle a salient part of his mood.* 8. See Daniel Henry, *Der Weg zum Kubismus*, Munich, Delphin Verlag, 1920 and Daniel Henry Kahnweiler, *Juan Gris*, New York, Buchholz, 1947. 9. Braque also did a smaller version with fewer houses. It is in the collection of Roger Dutilleul, Paris. 10. In *Mercure de France*, January 16, 1909. 11. *Gil Blas*, May 25, 1909. Described at some length in Henry: *Der Weg zum Kubismus*. 12. Alfred H. Barr, Jr., *Picasso: Fifty Years of His Art*, New York, Museum of Modern Art, 1946, p. 66. 13. Braque did a smaller version in which a palette hangs on a *trompe l'oeil* nail. 14. Author's hypothetical reconstruction. 15. A similar but slightly varied vertical composition of the *Café-Bar* is in the collection of Mr. and Mrs. Walter C. Arensberg, Hollywood, California. On the opposite side of the picture there is a large collage, probably of about the same date, 1918. 16. Letter dated February 17, 1930, in Kahnweiler, *Juan Gris*, p. 15. 17. See bibl. 29. 18. Douglas Cooper, *Braque*, London, Lindsay Drummond, 1948. 19. The date of these panels, which are in a private collection in France, is not certain. Braque thinks they were done in 1921 but Paul Rosenberg feels sure that they are later, perhaps 1923 or 1924. 20. Opened at Monte Carlo, January 19, 1924. Music by Georges Auric. 21. See bibl. 82. 22. I am indebted to Professor Otto Brendel for this information and other valuable observations about Braque's sources. 23. Although the apartment has since changed hands, the decorations still exist. 24. From a conversation reported by E. Teriade, *Minotaure*, No. 3-4, 1933, p. 10-11. 25. André Warnod in *Arts*, December 26, 1947.

CATALOG OF THE EXHIBITION

A **star preceding** the title indicates that the work is illustrated. Unless otherwise indicated, height precedes width.

PAINTINGS

1 The Port, 1904. Oil on canvas, 15 x 18½". Lent by Walter P. Chrysler, Jr., Warrenton, Virginia.

*2 Port at Antwerp, 1906. Oil on canvas, 15 x 18⅛". Lent by Baron Von der Heydt, Ascona, Switzerland. *Reproduced in color p. 19*

*3 Landscape at L'Estaque, 1906. Oil on canvas, 28¾ x 23⅝". Lent by Georges Grammont, Paris. *Ill. p. 21*

*4 Large Nude, 1907. Oil on canvas, 55¾ x 40". Lent by Mme Marie Cuttoli, Paris. *Ill. p. 26*

*5 Houses at L'Estaque, 1908. Oil on canvas, 28¾ x 23⅝". Lent by Hermann Rupf, Berne, Switzerland. *Reproduced in color p. 31*

*6 Port in Normandy, 1909. Oil on canvas, 32 x 32". Lent by Walter P. Chrysler, Jr., Warrenton, Virginia. *Ill. p. 35*

*7 Guitar and Compote Dish, 1909. Oil on canvas, 28¾ x 23⅝". Lent by Hermann Rupf, Berne, Switzerland. *Ill. p. 40*

*8 La Roche-Guyon with Tower, 1909. Oil on canvas, 28¾ x 23⅝". Lent by Roger Dutilleul, Paris. *Ill. p. 41*

*9 Still Life with Violin and Pitcher, 1909-10. Oil on canvas, 46½ x 28¾". Private collection, Paris. *Ill. p. 42*

*10 Woman with a Mandolin, 1910. Oil on canvas, 36 x 28½". Lent by Walter P. Chrysler, Jr., Warrenton, Virginia. *Ill. p. 45*

*11 Battleship, 1910-11. Oil on canvas, 31½ x 23". Private collection. *Ill. p. 50*

*12 Man with a Guitar, 1911. Oil on canvas, 45¾ x 31⅞". The Museum of Modern Art, New York. Acquired through the Lillie P. Bliss Bequest. *Ill. p. 47*

*13 The Portuguese, 1911. Oil on canvas, 46¼ x 28¾". Private collection, Paris. *Ill. p. 46*

*14 Collage with Newspaper, 1914. Pasted paper and pencil on board, 28¼ x 39¾". Lent by the Buchholz Gallery, New York. *Ill. p. 57*

*15 Glass and Violin, 1912. Pasted paper and oil on canvas, 45¾ x 31⅞". Private collection, Paris. *Ill. p. 63*

16 The Kubelick Poster, 1912. Oil on canvas, 18⅛ x 24". Private collection, Paris.

*17 Still Life with Playing Cards, 1913. Gouache and pasted paper on canvas, 31½ x 23¼". Lent by the Musée National d'Art Moderne, Paris. *Ill. p. 55*

*18 *Le Courrier*, 1913. Pasted paper on board, 20 x 22½". Courtesy Mr. Gallatin: A. E. Gallatin Collection, The Philadelphia Museum of Art. *Ill. p. 58*

*19 Black and White Collage, 1913. Pasted paper, charcoal and white chalk on paper, 24½ x 18⅞". Lent by Miss Katherine S. Dreier, Milford, Connecticut. *Ill. p. 56*

*20 The Clarinet, 1913. Pasted paper, charcoal, chalk and oil on canvas, 37½ x 47⅜". Lent by Amédée J. Ozenfant, New York. *Ill. p. 59*

*21 Woman with Guitar, 1913. Oil on canvas, 51¼ x 29⅛". Private collection, Paris. *Ill. p. 67*

*22 Musical Score, 1913. Oil on canvas, 25⅝ x 36¼". Private collection, Paris. *Ill. p. 66*

*23 Still Life on Table, 1913. Oil on canvas, 23⅝ x 28¾". Private collection, Paris. *Ill. p. 65*

*24 Guitar, 1913-14. Oil on canvas with pasted paper, pencil and chalk, 39¼ x 25⅝". The Museum of Modern Art, New York. Acquired through the Lillie P. Bliss Bequest. *Ill. p. 61*

*25 Music, 1914. Oil on canvas, 36 x 23½". Lent by Miss Katherine S. Dreier, Milford, Connecticut. *Ill. p. 71*

*26 Oval Still Life (*Le violon*), 1914. Oil on canvas, 36⅜ x 25¾". The Museum of Modern Art, New York. Gift of the Advisory Committee. *Ill. p. 69*

27 The Guitarist, 1914. Oil on canvas, 51 x 28¾". Lent by André Lefebvre, Paris.

28 The Daily, 1914. Collage, 41¾ x 29". Lent by André Lefebvre, Paris.

*29 Woman with a Mandolin, 1917. Oil on canvas, 36¼ x 25⅝". Lent by Roger Dutilleul, Paris. *Ill. p. 73*

*30 The Goblet, 1917-18. Oil on cardboard, 24 x 18". Courtesy Mr. Gallatin: A. E. Gallatin Collection, The Philadelphia Museum of Art. *Ill. p. 72*

*31 Still Life with Grapes, 1918. Oil on canvas, 19 x 25". Lent by Miss Marion G. Hendrie, Cincinnati. *Ill. p. 75*

*32 Rum Bottle, 1918. Oil on canvas, 38¾ x 27½". Lent by Mr. and Mrs. Joseph Pulitzer, Jr., St. Louis. *Ill. p. 76*

33 Still Life, 1918. Oil on canvas, 22 x 36⅝". Lent by Mme Jacques Doucet, Neuilly-sur-Seine, France. Courtesy C. de Hauke.

*34 The Musician, 1918. Oil on canvas, 90⅞ x 43½". Private collection, Paris. *Ill. p. 78*

*35 Still Life on Table, 1918. Oil on canvas, 51¼ x 29⅛". Private collection, Paris. *Ill. p. 84*

*36 On the Table, 1919. Oil and sand on canvas, 23 x 45". Lent by Mr. and Mrs. Joseph Pulitzer, Jr., St. Louis. *Reproduced in color p. 85*

*37 Still Life with Guitar, 1919. Oil on canvas, 28¾ x 45¾". Lent by Dr. E. Friedrich, Zurich. *Ill. p. 83*

*38 The Compote, 1919. Oil on canvas, 19¾ x 36¼″. Private collection, Paris. *Ill. p. 82*

39 Still Life: *Le Guéridon Noir*, 1919. Oil on canvas, 51¼ x 29½″. Private collection, Paris.

*40 Café-Bar, 1919. Oil on canvas, 63¼ x 31⅞″. Private collection, Paris. *Reproduced in color p. 79*

*41 The Buffet, 1919. Oil on canvas, 31⅞ x 39½″. Private collection, Paris. *Ill. p. 77*

*42 The Mantelpiece, 1922. Oil on canvas, 50 x 30″. Lent by Mr. and Mrs. Samuel A. Marx, Chicago. *Ill. p. 89*

*43 Figs and Grapes, 1922. Oil and sand on canvas, 7½ x 25½″. Private collection, New York. *Ill. p. 92*

*44 Still Life, 1923. Oil on canvas, 25½ x 30″. Lent by the Albright Art Gallery, Buffalo, New York. Room of Contemporary Art. *Ill. p. 102*

*45 Nude with Basket of Fruit, 1924. Oil on canvas, 36 x 28″. Lent by Wright Ludington, Santa Barbara, California. *Ill. p. 95*

46 Woman with Basket, 1924. Red chalk on wood, 19¾ x 16½″. Lent by Dr. G. F. Reber and Frau Erna Reber, Chailly-sur-Lausanne, Vaud, Switzerland.

47 Sugar Bowl with Fruit, 1924. Oil on canvas, 8 x 25½″. Lent by Georges de Batz & Company, New York.

*48 Anemones, 1925. Oil and sand on canvas, 19½ x 24″. Private collection, New York. *Ill. p. 100*

*49 Woman with Basket of Fruit, 1926. Oil on canvas, 63½ x 29″. Chester Dale Collection. The Art Institute of Chicago loan. *Ill. p. 96*

*50 Still Life with Grapes, 1927. Oil on canvas, 21 x 29″. Lent by The Phillips Gallery, Washington, D. C. *Ill. p. 106*

*51 The Mantelpiece, 1927. Oil on canvas, 51½ x 29¼″. Lent by the Norton Gallery and School of Art, West Palm Beach, Florida. *Ill. p. 101*

*52 Mussels and Oysters, 1927. Oil and sand on canvas, 10¼ x 26⅞″. Private collection, New York. *Ill. p. 99*

*53 Guitar, Fruit and Pitcher, 1927. Oil and sand on canvas, 29 x 36″. Lent by Mr. and Mrs. M. Lincoln Schuster, New York. *Ill. p. 105*

*53a Black Rose, 1927. Oil on canvas, 20 x 37″. Lent by Mrs. Burton Tremaine, Jr., The Miller Company, Meriden, Connecticut. *Reproduced in color p. 103*

*54 Still Life: The Table, 1928. Oil on canvas, 32 x 53″. Chester Dale Collection. The Art Institute of Chicago loan. *Ill. p. 107*

*55 The Table (*Le guéridon*), 1928. Oil on canvas, 71 x 28¾″. Lent by Walter P. Chrysler, Jr., Warrenton, Virginia. *Ill. p. 108*

*56 Still Life, 1928. Oil on canvas, 19¼ x 35½″. Lent by Mr. and Mrs. John Rood, Minneapolis. *Ill. p. 111*

*57 The Table, 1928. Oil on canvas, 70¾ x 28¾″. The Museum of Modern Art, New York. Acquired through the Lillie P. Bliss Bequest. *Reproduced in color p. 109*

*58 The Round Table, 1929. Oil on canvas, 58 x 45″. Lent by The Phillips Gallery, Washington, D. C. *Ill. p. 112*

59 Glass and Fruit, Marble Table, 1929. Oil and sand on canvas, 15¾ x 47½″. Lent by Mr. and Mrs. Henry R. Hope, Bloomington, Indiana.

*60 Cliffs and Fishing Boat, 1929. Oil on canvas, 13 x 18″. Private collection, New York. *Ill. p. 115*

*61 The Crystal Vase, 1929. Oil on canvas, 16 x 48¼″. Private collection, New York. *Ill. p. 111*

*62 The Blue Mandolin, 1930. Oil on canvas, 46¼ x 34⅝″. Lent by the City Art Museum of St. Louis. *Ill. p. 117*

*63 The Table (*Le guéridon*), 1930. Oil on canvas, 57⅝ x 30⅜″. Lent by Mr. and Mrs. Jacques Helft, Buenos Aires. *Ill. p. 116*

*64 Guitar and Bottle of Marc, 1930. Oil on canvas, 51¼ x 29″. Private collection, New York. *Color frontispiece*

*65 The Bathers, 1931. Oil on canvas, 51½ x 77″. Lent by Walter P. Chrysler, Jr., Warrenton, Virginia. *Ill. p. 121*

*66 The Red Tablecloth, 1931. Oil on canvas, 34¾ x 45¼″. Lent by Mrs. Edna K. Warner, Fort Lauderdale, Florida. *Ill. p. 122*

*67 The Clay Pipe, 1931. Oil on canvas, 10¾ x 13¾″. The Museum of Modern Art, New York. *Ill. p. 118*

*68 Apples, 1933. Oil on canvas, 35 x 45¾″. Lent by Walter P. Chrysler, Jr., Warrenton, Virginia. *Ill. p. 120*

*69 The Pink Tablecloth, 1933. Oil and sand on canvas, 38⅛ x 51¼″. Lent by Walter P. Chrysler, Jr., Warrenton, Virginia. *Reproduced in color p. 125*

*70 The Yellow Tablecloth, 1935. Oil on canvas, 45 x 57″. Lent by Mr. and Mrs. Samuel A. Marx, Chicago. *Ill. p. 124*

*71 Woman with a Mandolin, 1937. Oil on canvas, 51¼ x 38¼″. The Museum of Modern Art, New York. Mrs. Simon Guggenheim Fund. *Reproduced in color p. 129*

*72 The Cliffs, 1938. Oil on canvas, 19¾ x 25¾″. Lent by Mr. and Mrs. Leigh B. Block, Chicago. *Ill. p. 127*

*73 Pitcher, Bread and Lemon, 1939. Oil on canvas, 18 x 22″. Lent by Mr. and Mrs. Leigh B. Block, Chicago. *Ill. p. 132*

*74 Painter and Model, 1939. Oil on canvas, 51 x 69″. Lent by Walter P. Chrysler, Jr., Warrenton, Virginia. *Ill. p. 128*

*75 The Studio, 1939. Oil on canvas, 45 x 57½″. Lent by Paul Rosenberg, New York. *Ill. p. 131*

76 Still Life with Garden Chair, 1940. Oil on canvas, 26 x 32″. Lent by Mr. and Mrs. Otto L. Spaeth, New York.

*77 Kitchen Still Life, 1942. Oil on canvas, 65⅛ x 31½″. Lent by Jean Paulhan, Paris. *Ill. p. 140*

*78 The Blue Wash Basin, 1942. Oil on canvas, 23½ x 31½". Lent by Mr. and Mrs. Abner Goldstone, New York. *Ill. p. 138*

*79 Flowers on Box, 1942. Oil on canvas, 34 x 24". Lent by Mr. and Mrs. Leo Glass, New York. *Ill. p. 142*

*80 The Green Tablecloth, 1943. Oil on canvas, 18⅛ x 24¾". Lent by the Musée National d'Art Moderne, Paris. *Ill. p. 146*

*81 The Stove, 1944. Oil on canvas, 57⅝ x 35". Lent by the Galerie Maeght, Paris. *Ill. p. 147*

*82 The Salon, 1944. Oil on canvas, 47⅜ x 58¾". Lent by the Musée National d'Art Moderne, Paris. *Reproduced in color p. 143*

*83 The Sunflowers, 1946. Oil on canvas, 41¼ x 41¼". Lent by The Reader's Digest, Pleasantville, New York. *Ill. p. 151*

*84 Still Life with Flowers, 1946. Oil on canvas, 34¾ x 43". Lent by Stephen C. Clark, New York. *Ill. p. 150*

*85 The Chair, 1947. Oil on canvas, 25⅝ x 19". Lent by the Galerie Maeght, Paris. *Ill. p. 153*

DRAWINGS

*86 Compote and Guitar, 1920. Red chalk on paper, 26¾ x 34¼". Lent by Hermann Rupf, Berne, Switzerland. *Ill. p. 91*

*87 Seated Nude, 1924. Black chalk on paper, 35½ x 28¾". Lent by Dr. G. F. Reber and Frau Erna Reber, Chailly-sur-Lausanne, Vaud, Switzerland. *Ill. p. 94*

*88 Nude, c. 1924. Pencil and chalk on paper, 15 x 26". Lent by Louis E. Stern, New York. *Ill. p. 97*

*89 Apples, 1934. Red chalk on paper, 19½ x 26½". Lent by Richard S. Davis, Wayzata, Minnesota. *Ill. p. 121*

*90 The Chair, 1946. Charcoal on paper, 18½ x 24". Lent by David Mann, New York. *Ill. p. 152*

PRINTS AND ILLUSTRATIONS

91 Job, 1912. Drypoint, 5⅞ x 7⅞". The Museum of Modern Art, New York. Gift of Victor S. Riesenfeld.

*92 Fox, 1912. Drypoint, 21½ x 15". The Museum of Modern Art, New York. *Ill. p. 156*

93 Guitar and Case, 1921. Color woodcut, 3¼ x 4¼". The Museum of Modern Art, New York. One of three color woodcuts for Erik Satie's *Le Piège de Méduse*. Published by the Galerie Simon (Kahnweiler), Paris, 1921.

94 Still Life, 1922. Color lithograph, 8 x 15⅝". The Museum of Modern Art, New York. Gift of Mrs. Saidie A. May.

95 *Les Fâcheux*, 1924. The Museum of Modern Art, New York. Color reproductions of décor and costumes for the Diaghilev ballet produced in 1924. Published by the Editions des Quatres chemins, Paris, 1924.

96 Earth, c.1932. Etching, 14½ x 11¾". Lent by the Buchholz Gallery, New York. This and the following two etchings are from a series of sixteen illustrations commissioned by Ambroise Vollard to illustrate Hesiod's *Theogony*.

97 Hera and Themis, c.1932. Etching, 14½ x 11¾". Lent by the Buchholz Gallery, New York.

*98 Goddess on Horseback, c.1932. Etching, 14½ x 11¾". The Museum of Modern Art, New York. *Ill. p. 156*

*99 Io, 1945. Color lithograph, 12⅛ x 17". The Museum of Modern Art, New York. Acquired through the Lillie P. Bliss Bequest. *Ill. p. 159*

*100 Helios (I), 1946. Lithograph, trial proof, 10⅝ x 9⅛". The Museum of Modern Art, New York. Gift of Victor S. Riesenfeld. *Ill. p. 157*

101 Helios (II), 1946. Color lithograph, trial proof, 14 x 11½". The Museum of Modern Art, New York. Gift of Victor S. Riesenfeld.

*102 Helios (IV), 1947. Color lithograph, 20 x 16¾". Lent by James William Reid, New York. *Ill. p. 157*

*103 Teapot and Lemon, 1947. Color lithograph, 14⅜ x 21¾". Lent by the Buchholz Gallery, N. Y. *Ill. p. 158*

104 *Cahier de Georges Braque*, 1947. Selections of maxims from Braque's notebooks (1917-47) written in the artist's hand with marginal decorations and reproduced in facsimile. Published by the Galerie Maeght, Paris, 1948.

SCULPTURE, PLASTERS, ETC.

105 Palette of the Artist. Lent by the Galerie Pierre, Paris.

*106 Figure, 1920. Plaster, 7¾" high. Lent by the Buchholz Gallery, New York. *Ill. p. 93*

*107 The Pony, 1939. Bronze, 7¼" high. Lent by Wright Ludington, Santa Barbara, California. *Ill. p. 134*

*107a Io, 1939. Plaster relief, 8⅝ x 10¾". Lent by Dr. and Mrs. F. R. Hensel, Indianapolis. *Ill. p. 135*

108 The Bird, 1940. Engraved plaster, 12½ x 9½". Lent by the artist.

*109 Fish, 1942. Bronze, 14" long. Lent by the Buchholz Gallery, New York. *Ill. p. 133*

110 The Hunt, 1943. Bronze relief, 12 x 9". Lent by the Buchholz Gallery, New York.

*111 Head of a Horse, 1946? Bronze, 38½" long. Lent by the Buchholz Gallery, New York. *Ill. p. 133*

112 Uranie, 1946. Engraved plaster, 8⅞ x 11¾". Lent by the Galerie Maeght, Paris.

113 Profile Head. Bronze, 13¼" high. Lent by the artist.

114 Vase. Bronze, 11⅝" high. Lent by the artist.

EXHIBITIONS (One-man and important groups)

1906 Paris. *Salon des Indépendants.* 7 works
1907 Paris. *Salon des Indépendants.* 6 works
Paris. *Salon d'Automne.* 1 work
1908 Paris. Galerie Kahnweiler. Nov. 9-28. 27 works
1909 Paris. *Salon des Indépendants.* 2 works
1913 New York, Chicago, Boston. Association of American Painters and Sculptors (Armory Show) Feb.-May. 3 works. (First U.S. showing)
1914 Dresden. Galerie Emile Richter. Spring. 38 works
Berlin. Galerie Feldmann. Spring. 38 works as above
New York. Photo-Secession Gallery. Dec. 9-Jan. 9, 1915. (With Picasso)
1919 Paris. Galerie Léonce Rosenberg. Mar. 5-31
1920 Paris. *Salon des Indépendants.* 4 works
Paris. *Salon d'Automne.* 3 works
1921 Paris. Hotel Drouot. Uhde Sale. May 30. 17 works
Paris. Hotel Drouot. Kahnweiler Sale, 1st part. June 13-14. 22 works
Paris. Hotel Drouot. Kahnweiler Sale, 2nd part. Nov. 17-18. 38 works
1922 Paris. Hotel Drouot. Kahnweiler Sale, 3rd part. 18 works. July 4
Paris. *Salon d'Automne.* 18 works
1923 Paris. Hotel Drouot. Kahnweiler Sale, 4th part. 85 works. May 7
1924 Paris. Paul Rosenberg. May 2-21. 16 works
1925 Berlin. Galerie Flechtheim. March
Paris. Galerie Vivin-Raspail. December
1926 Paris. Paul Rosenberg. Mar. 8-27. 62 works
1929 Paris. Paul Rosenberg. May. (Group)
1930 Paris. Paul Rosenberg. May. (Group)
Berlin. Galerie Flechtheim. Sept. 21-mid October. 24 works (With Matisse and Picasso)
1931 New York. Museum of French Art. Feb. 5 works. (With Picasso and Léger)
1933 Basel. Kunsthalle. Apr. 9-May 14. 183 works
1934 New York. Durand-Ruel. Mar. 13-31. 13 works. (With Matisse and Picasso)
London, Alex. Reid & Lefevre. July. 41 works
New York. Valentine Gallery. Nov. 26-Dec. 15. 16 works
1935 Paris. "Beaux Arts" & "Gazette des Beaux Arts." Mar.-Apr. 25 works (Group)
1936 Paris. Paul Rosenberg. Jan. 8-31. 20 works
London. Rosenberg & Helft, Ltd. Oct. 15-mid November. 14 works. (With Matisse and Picasso)
New York. Museum of Modern Art. Mar. 2-Apr. 19. 9 works. (Cubism and abstract art exhibition)
Brussels. Palais des Beaux Arts. Nov.-Dec. 81 works
1937 Paris. Paul Rosenberg. Jan. 6-30. (With Matisse and Picasso)
Paris. Paul Rosenberg. Apr. 3-30. 18 works
Paris. Petit Palais. June-Oct. 29 works. (*Maitres de l'art indépendant*)
1938 Stockholm. Liljevalchs Konsthall. 38 works (Group). Also shown at Oslo, Copenhagen and Göteborg

London. Rosenberg & Helft, Ltd. July. 22 works
New York. Buchholz Gallery. Oct. 14-29. 16 works
Paris. Paul Rosenberg. Nov. 16-Dec. 10. 22 works
1939 Paris. Paul Rosenberg. Apr. 4-29. 27 works
London. Rosenberg & Helft, Ltd. June 6-July 8. 24 works
Chicago. Arts Club. Nov. 7-27. 68 works
Washington, D.C. Phillips Memorial Gallery. Dec. 6-Jan. 6, 1940. 55 works, as shown in Chicago
1940 San Francisco. Museum of Art. Feb. 6-Mar. 3. Mostly as shown in Chicago, Washington. 67 works
1941 Richmond. Virginia Museum of Fine Arts. Jan. 6-Mar. 4. 15 works. (Chrysler collection) Also shown in Philadelphia
New York. Valentine Gallery. Jan. 13-Feb. 8. 27 works
1942 New York. Paul Rosenberg. Apr. 7-25. 13 works
Baltimore. Museum of Art. Nov. 22-Dec. 27. 16 works
1943 New York. Paul Rosenberg. Apr. 6-May 1. 6 works (With Picasso)
Paris. *Salon d'Automne.* Sept. 25-Oct. 31. 35 works
1944 Paris. *Salon d'Automne.* Oct. 6-Nov. 5. 2 works
New York. Paul Rosenberg. Nov. 6-Dec. 2. 4 works
1945 Paris. Galerie de France. May 25-June 30. 9 works (*Le Cubisme*)
Philadelphia. Museum of Art. June-Nov. 9 works (With Picasso and Léger)
Amsterdam. Stedelijk Museum. Oct. 20-Nov. 12. 26 works
Brussels. Palais des Beaux Arts. Nov. 24-Dec. 13. 27 works, mostly as shown in Amsterdam
1946 New York. Paul Rosenberg. Apr. 29-May 18. 11 works
London. Tate Gallery. May. 28 works. (With Rouault)
Chicago. Art Institute. June 28-Sept. 30. 5 works. (With Picasso)
Zurich. Kunsthaus. Sept. 21-Oct. 20. 26 works, mostly as shown in London. (With Picasso and Kandinsky)
1947 Paris. Galerie Maeght. June. 58 works
Avignon. Palais des Papes. June 27-Sept. 30. 13 works. (Group exhibition)
New York. Seligmann-Helft. November
1948 New York. Paul Rosenberg. Jan. 5-24. 15 works
Basel. Kunsthalle. Feb. 26-Mar. 24. 40 works. (With Picasso and Gris)
Berne. Kunsthalle. Apr. 2-29. 37 works, mostly as shown in Basel
Paris. Galerie Maeght. June. (Graphic works)
Venice. Biennale. May-Oct. 18 works
Venice. Galleria d'Arte del Cavallino. July. (Graphic works as shown in Paris)
Chaux de Fonds
Zurich. Kunsthaus. Aug. 20-mid September. (With Picasso and Gris, 25 works
Geneva. Athénee. September
Basel. Galerie d'Art Moderne. October

BIBLIOGRAPHY

Statements by the artist are arranged chronologically, interviews alphabetically by interviewer, and material about the artist alphabetically by author, or by title in the case of unsigned articles and compilations. Exhibition catalogs are grouped by city, and listed chronologically under the names of the respective galleries. Catalogs of collections (Chrysler, Gallatin, etc.) which have been exhibited appear, however, under the names of the collections in the main portion of the bibliography. Exhibition reviews have been included in the exhibition catalog section with cross references to more generally critical, related articles listed under their authors' names in the body of the bibliography.

Inclusion in the exhibition catalog section has been limited to one-man and important group exhibition catalogs, and to material accessible to the compiler, although additional catalogs have doubtless been published. Numerous exhibition reviews appearing in newspapers and general periodicals, usually concurrent with the exhibition, have also not been mentioned. Omitted, too, are general art histories, etc. which contain mere mention of the artist's name.

Abbreviations used: Ap April, Ag August, Aufl. Auflage, bibl. this bibliography, col colored, D December, ed editor, edition, edited, F February, il illustration(s), Ja January, Je June, Jy July, Mr March, My May, N November, n. d. not dated, no number(s), O October, p page(s), passim in various places, por portrait(s), S September, [ ] information supplied by compiler, * material may be found in Museum of Modern Art Library, † material has not been examined by compiler.

Sample entry explained: AMBLER, JACQUELIN. The Gallic traditionalism of Braque. il Bulletin, City Art Museum (St. Louis) 20no1-2:2-4 Ap 1945 means that an article entitled the Gallic traditionalism of Braque, accompanied by illustrations, will be found in the Bulletin of the City Art Museum of St. Louis, volume 20, number 1-2, pages 2-4 of the April 1945 issue.

HANNAH B. MULLER

STATEMENTS BY BRAQUE

*1 PENSÉES ET RÉFLEXIONS SUR LA PEINTURE. Nord-Sud (Paris) no10:3-5 D 1917.
* Reprinted in bibl. 115; translated into English in Robert Goldwater and Marco Treves, ed. Artists on art. p421-3 New York, Pantheon Books, 1945 and in bibl. 85; reprinted with the deletion of one paragraph
* in German in Kunstblatt 4: 49-51 1920 and in Paul
* Westheim. Künstlerbekenntnisse. p148-9 Berlin, Propyläen Verlag [n.d.] Excerpts reprinted in bibl. 40,148.
*2 PENSÉES. Valori Plastici (Rome) 1no2-3:2 F-Mr 1919.
7 epigrams quoted in a letter about cubism from Léonce Rosenberg to the editor of Valori Plastici. 6 of these are reprinted in bibl. 1.

*3 TESTIMONY AGAINST GERTRUDE STEIN. p13-14 The Hague, Servire Press, 1935. (Transition pamphlet. no1).
Published as supplement to Transition 1934-1935 (no23). Reaction against Autobiography of Alice B. Toklas by Gertrude Stein.
*4 [RÉPONSE À UNE ENQUÊTE] il Cahiers d'Art 10:21-2, 24 1935.
According to conversations with Christian Zervos. Reproductions of Braque's work, p20,23,25-7,29-30 of same issue.
*5 REFLECTIONS. il Verve 1no2:7 Spring 1938.
English translation of statements selected from the artist's notebooks. 3 col plates, p53,56 of same issue.
*6 [RÉPONSE À UNE ENQUÊTE] Cahiers d'Art 14:65-7 1939.
*7 [STATEMENTS BY BRAQUE] col il Verve 2no8:56-7 S-N 1940.
From the artist's notebooks.
*8 [RÉPONSE À UNE ENQUÊTE DE "LETTRES FRANÇAISES" À PROPOS DE "L'ART ET LE PUBLIC"] Lettres Françaises (Paris) Mr 15 1946.
*9 [FRAGMENTS INÉDITS DES] CAHIERS DE BRAQUE. Amour de l'Art 26:3 Ja 1946.
Drawing from Braque's notebook, p2 of same issue.
10 ALBUM DU PEINTRE. il Saisons (Paris) no3:25-31 Winter 1946-7.
*11 CAHIER DE GEORGES BRAQUE, 1917-1947. 93p il Paris, Maeght, 1948.
Includes statements also in bibl. 1, 2, 5, 7, 9, 10, 110, 172.
12 TÉMOIGNAGE. il K; revue de la poésie (Paris) no1-2:11 Je 1948.

INTERVIEWS WITH BRAQUE

*13 DIEHL, GASTON. L'univers pictural et son destin: extrait d'une conversation avec Georges Braque. *In* Gaston Diehl, ed. Les problèmes de la peinture. p307-9 Paris, Editions Confluences, 1945.
*14 JEDLICKA, GOTTHARD. Begegnung mit Georges Braque. *In* the author's Begegnungen: Künstlernovellen. p127-52 il por Basel, Benno Schwabe, 1933.
Reprinted in 2d enlarged edition published by Eugen Rentsch, Erlenbach-Zurich, 1945, p92-111.
*15 RYDBECK-ZUHR, INGRID. Samtal i en ateljé. il Konstrevy (Stockholm) 23hft4:202-10 1947.
*16 TÉRIADE, E. Emancipation de la peinture. il (some col) Minotaure no3-4:9-20 1933.
*17 WARNOD, ANDRÉ. Tous les *ismes* conduisent au conformisme, nous déclare Braque. il Arts no146:1, 5 D 26 1947.
*18 ——— Braque . . . s'est remis au travail. il Arts no55:1,3 F 15 1946.
——— See also 110.

BOOKS, ARTICLES

*19 AMBLER, JAQUELIN. The Gallic traditionalism of Braque. il Bulletin, City Art Museum (St. Louis) 20no1-2:2-4 Ap 1945.
Includes analysis of *The Blue Mandolin* acquired by City Art Museum. Acquisition also mentioned in Pictures on Exhibit 6:39 F 1945 and in Art Digest 19:8 Ja 15 1945.

*20 ANALYTICAL BRAQUE, STILL LIFE, PRESENTED TO HONOLULU. il Art Digest 15:6 S 1941.

†21 APOLLINAIRE, GUILLAUME. [Preface to catalog of Braque exhibition, Kahnweiler Gallery] N 1908.
Excerpt reprinted in bibl.142.

†22 ——— [Georges Braque] Mercure de France Ja 16 1909.
Reprinted in bibl.76.

†23 ——— [Georges Braque] Revue Indépendante, pl66, Ag 1911.
Reprinted in bibl.76.

*24 ——— Les peintres cubistes. p40-2 Paris, Figuière, 1913. (Tous les arts)
(Reprinted in bibl.76. Translated into German in Querschnitt 7:192-3 Mr. 1927.

*25 BAKER, SARAH. Georges Braque. il Right Angle (Washington, D.C.) 1no5:4-5 Jy 1947.

*26 BASLER, ADOLPHE & KUNSTLER, CHARLES. The modernists from Matisse to de Segonzac. p44-5 il New York, W. Farquhar Payson, 1931.
Brief comment.

27 BAZIN, GERMAIN. Braque 1939. il Prométhée 20:179-81 Je 1939.
Occasioned by exhibition held at Galerie Rosenberg, Paris, Ap 1939.
——— See also 160.

28 BILL, MAX. Braque, Kandinsky, Picasso. Arts no100:8 Ja 3 1947.
Review of exhibition, Kunsthaus, Zurich.

*29 BILLE, EJLER. Georges Braque. *In* the author's Picasso, surrealisme, abstrakt kunst. p68-74 il Kφbenhavn, Helios, 1945.

†30 BISSIÈRE, ROGER. Exposition Braque. Opinion Mr 29 1919.

31 ——— Georges Braque: vingt tableaux. 1re série. 6p plus 20 plates Paris, Editions de l'Effort moderne (Léonce Rosenberg) 1920. (Les Maîtres du cubisme)
* Text reprinted in Bulletin de l'Effort Moderne
* no3:11-14 Mr 1924; in Art d'Aujourd'hui 2no6:21-5 été 1925; and in bibl.76.

*32 BONFANTE, EGIDIO & RAVENNA, JUTI. Georges Braque. *In* their Arte cubista. p107-31 il (some col) Venezia, Ateneo, 1945.
Brief text, 11 illustrations.

33 BONJEAN, JACQUES. L'époque fauve de Braque. il Beaux Arts 75no268:4 F 18 1938.
Review of exhibition, Galerie Pierre, Paris.

*34 BOVE, EMMANUEL. Georges Braque. il (some col) Formes (Paris) no3:4-5 Mr 1930.

*35 BRANDT, BILL. [Photograph of Georges Braque and of Braque's lectern] il Verve 1no2:52,55 Spring 1938. |

*36 BRAQUE. por Harper's Bazaar 80no3:156-7 Mr 1946.
Photographs of Braque in his studio by Brassai.

*37 BRAQUE JOINS AMERICANS IN NORTON GALLERY ACCESSIONS. il Art News 46:39 Ap 1947.
Braque's *Mantel* acquired.

*38 BRAQUE LITHOGRAPH; STILL-LIFE WITH APPLE. il Art News 46:10 O 1947.
Includes analysis of lithograph.

*39 BRETON, ANDRÉ. Le surréalisme et la peinture. p33-6 New York, Brentano's, 1945.
First published in 1928 in Paris by Editions de la Nouvelle revue française.
Reprinted in bibl. 76.

*40 BULLIET, CLARENCE J. The significant moderns and their pictures. p88-91 il New York, Covici Friede, 1936.
Includes statements by Braque, reprinted from bibl. 1.

*41 BURGER, FRITZ. Cézanne und Hodler: Einführung in die Probleme der Malerei der Gegenwart. 1:122;2:136 il München, Delphin Verlag, 1919.
Brief analysis of *Lady with a Mandolin*.

*42 CASSOU, JEAN. Georges Braque. il Cahiers d'Art 3no1:5-11 1928.

43 ——— Braque, Marcoussis et Juan Gris. il por Amour de l'Art 14:227-33 N 1933.
Reprinted in bibl. 89.

44 ———Oeuvres récentes de Braque. il Amour de l'Art 11:80-90 1930.

45 ———Le secret de Braque. il Amour de l'Art 26:4-8 Ja 1946.
——— See also 76.

†46 CENDRARS, BLAISE. Braque. Rose Rouge Je 19 1919.
Reprinted in Le Centaure 3no9:244 Je 1929, and in bibl. 76.

†47 CÈPE, P. [Georges Braque] Paris Journal Ap 13 1923.
CHAR, RENÉ. See 173.

48 CHRYSLER, WALTER P., JR. COLLECTION. Collection of Walter P. Chrysler, Jr. exhibited . . . by Virginia museum of fine arts . . . Philadelphia museum of art. 154p il Richmond, 1941.
Includes 15 paintings by Braque, p24-33. Text by Henry McBride.

*49 COGNIAT, RAYMOND. Braque. il Arts no118:1 Je 6 1947.
Occasioned by exhibition held at Galerie Maeght, Paris.

50 ——— Braque et les ballets russes. il Amour de l'Art 12:206-8 My 1931.
Discusses designs for *Les Fâcheux*, *Zéphyr et Flore* and *Salade*.
——— See also 171, 180.
COOPER, DOUGLAS. See 83,98.

*51 COQUIOT, GUSTAVE. Braque. *In* the author's Cubistes, futuristes, passéistes. [Nouvelle éd.] p7-8 il Paris, Ollendorff, 1923.

*52 COURTHION, PIERRE. Panorama de la peinture française contemporaine. p113-16 il Paris, Kra, 1927.
An extract is reprinted in Le Centaure 1no10:184-5 Jy 1927
DIEHL, GASTON. See 13.

*53 DORIVAL, BERNARD. Braque. *In* the author's Les peintres célèbres. p332-3 il por Paris, Mazenod, 1948.
Stylistic analysis, in part, chronological. Volume includes frontispiece especially designed by Braque.

*54 ―――― Les dons [au Musée national d'art moderne, Paris] il Musées de France (Paris) p172-80 juillet 1948.
Braque's *Les poissons noirs* discussed, p178-9.
―――― See also 172.

*55 DU COLOMBIER, PIERRE & MANUEL, ROLAND. Les arts. passim il Paris, Denoël et Steele, 1933.
Scattered comments on Braque in relation to other artists.

*56 DUVAL, RÉMY, photographer. Intimités de Braque. il por Amour de l'Art 27no5:215-18 1947.
Photograph of Braque, his hand, his studio, his paint pots and brushes.

*57 EARP, T. W. The modern movement in painting. p33 col il London, The Studio, 1935.
EDE, H. S. See 76.

*58 EGLINGTON, LAURIE. Braque, Matisse, Picasso exhibited [at Durand-Ruel] il Art News 32no24:3-5 Mr 17 1934.
Review of exhibition. Braque, p4. Complete catalog listing 13 works by Braque, p5.

*59 EINSTEIN, CARL. Georges Braque. 140p il (some col) Paris, Editions des Chroniques du jour, 1934.
Excerpt reprinted in Beaux Arts 73no19:1,5 Jy 6 1934.

*60 ―――― Die Kunst des 20. Jahrhunderts. 2. Aufl. p88-91, 296-317 il (some col) Berlin, Propyläen Verlag, 1926.

*61 ―――― Tableaux récents de Georges Braque. il Documents 1:289-96 N 1929.
―――― See also 76, 150.

*62 ELUARD, PAUL. Georges Braque. *In* the author's Voir. p37-9 il(1col) Genève-Paris, Editions des Trois collines, 1948.

* Poem reprinted from the author's Capitale de la douleur. p128 Paris, Gallimard, 1926.

*63 ESCHOLIER, RAYMOND. La peinture française XXe siècle. p86-8 il Paris, Floury, 1937.

*64 FERNANDEZ, JUSTINO. Picasso y Braque. *In* the author's Prometeo. p25-8 il Mexico, D.F., Editorial Porrua, 1945.

*65 FIERENS, PAUL. Georges Braque. por Sélection (Antwerp) 3no4:360-2,400 F 1924.

*66 FRIED, ANNY. Braque. il Forum (Bratislava) 7no6: 115-16 1937.

*67 FUMET, STANISLAS. Braque. 14p il plus 24 col plates New York, Braun, 1945. (Couleurs des maîtres)

*68 ―――― Braque. 14p il plus 48 plates Paris, Braun, 194?. (Collection "Les Maîtres")

*69 GALLATIN, ALBERT E. Georges Braque; essay and bibliography. 26p plus 12 plates (1 col) por New York, Wittenborn, 1943.

*70 GALLATIN, ALBERT E. COLLECTION. Museum of living art, A. E. Gallatin collection, New York university. p12,22-3 il New York, 1940.
Includes 11 works by Braque. Critical notes by George L.K. Morris. Introduction by Jean Hélion. The collection is now in the Philadelphia Museum of Art.

71 GASCH, SEBASTIÀ. Georges Braque. L'Amic de les arts (Sitges) 2no12:31-2 Ap 1927.

*72 GEORGE, WALDEMAR. The artist's dilemma. il Formes no17:114 S 1931.

*73 ―――― Georges Braque. il (some col) Esprit Nouveau 1:638-56 1921.

74 ―――― Georges Braque. il Amour de l'Art 3:298-300 O 1922.

*75 GEORGES BRAQUE: A LEADER OF MODERN ART. il por Picture Post (London) 32no1:26-7 Jy 20 1946.

*76 GEORGES BRAQUE. il por Cahiers d'Art 8no1-2: 1-84 1933.
Issued on occasion of exhibition at Kunstmuseum, Basel. Includes text by Christian Zervos, G. Apollinaire (reprinted from bibl.22-4); A. Salmon (reprinted from bibl.121); Bissière (reprinted from bibl.31); B. Cendrars (reprinted from bibl.46); André Lhote (reprinted from bibl.102); A. Soffici (reprinted from bibl.123); J. Cassou; A. Breton (reprinted from bibl. 39); H. S. Ede, C. Einstein. 163 illustrations of Braque's work.

*77 GEORGES BRAQUE. OEUVRES RÉCENTES (GALERIE PAUL ROSENBERG) il Cahiers d'Art 12:96-9 1937.

*78 GIEDION-WELCKER, CAROLA. Braque, Kandinsky, Picasso. Werk 33:sup143 N 1946.
Review of exhibition, Kunsthaus, Zurich.

*79 GLEIZES, ALBERT. Du cubisme et des moyens de le comprendre. p12 Paris, "La Cible," 1920.

*80 ―――― Kubismus. passim il München A. Langen, 1928. (Bauhausbücher 13)
GOLDWATER, ROBERT. See 1.

*81 GORDON, JAN. Modern French painters. p143-4 il New York, Dodd, Mead, 1923.

82 GOTTLIEB, AURELIE. Repräsentative ausländische künstler. il Deutsche Kunst und Dekoration 64:3-5 Ap 1929.
Includes comments on Braque.

*83 GRENIER, JEAN. Braque, peintures, 1909-1947. 8p plus 16 col plates Paris, Les Editions du Chêne, 1948.
Same plates published with text by Douglas Cooper by Lindsay Drummond, Ltd., London and Les Editions du Chêne, Paris, 1948.

84 GROHMANN, WILL. Georges Braque. il Cicerone 21:576-82 1929.

*85 GUGGENHEIM, PEGGY, COLLECTION. Art of this century . . . 1910 to 1940, ed. by Peggy Guggenheim. p62-4 il New York, 1942.
Includes 1 work by Braque. Translation of Braque's statements from bibl.1.
HALVORSEN, WALTHER. See 179.
HÉLION, JEAN. See 70.
HENRY, DANIEL. See 96-8.

86 HERTZ, HENRI. Georges Braque et le réveil des apparences. Amour de l'Art 7:135-40 Ap 1926.
Occasioned by exhibition held at Galerie Rosenberg, Paris.

*87 HILDEBRANDT, H. Die Kunst des 19. und 20. Jahrhunderts. p391-2 il Wildpark-Potsdam, Akademische Verlagsgesellschaft Athenaion, 1924.

*88 HORTER, EARL. Abstract painting, a visit to Braque. Pennsylvania Museum Bulletin 29:62-3 Mr 1934.
* Reprinted in Art Digest 8:22 Ap 15 1934.

*89 HUYGHE, RENÉ. Les contemporains. p34 il (some col) Paris, Bibliothèque française des arts, 1939.
* Translated into English in the author's The contemporaries, New York, French and European Publications, 1939.

*90 ——, ed. Histoire de l'art contemporain: la peinture. passim il Paris, Alcan. 1935.
Reprinted from Amour de l'Art 14:209-40 N 1933. Includes biographical notes and bibliography.

†91 Isarlov, George. [Georges Braque] L'Annonciation, 1925.

92 —— Georges Braque. 31p Paris, Corti, 1932. (Collection Orbes)
* Also published in Orbes (Paris) no3:71-97 Spring 1932. Includes list of works, 1906-1929; exhibitions, 1906-1926; collections including works by Braque and a brief bibliography.

93 JAKOVSKI, ANATOLE. Georges Braque. il Arts de France no8:31-6 1946.

*94 JANNEAU, GUILLAUME. L'art cubiste, théories et réalisations. passim il Paris, Moreau, 1929.

*95 JEDLICKA, GOTTHARD. Matisse—Picasso—Braque. Werk 32:125-8 Ap 1945.
From a speech held at the Zurich Kunsthaus in O 1932. Published by Oprecht and Helbling, Zurich, 1934.
—— See also 14.

*96 KAHNWEILER, HENRY. Der Weg zum Kubismus. passim il München, Delphin Verlag, 1920.

*97 —— Werkstätten. Die Freude (Burg Lauenstein) 1:153-4 1920.
Brief description of Braque's studio, 1914. Illustrations of Braque's work, p64-5, 152-3 of same volume.

*98 —— Juan Gris, sa vie, son oeuvres, ses écrits. passim il Paris, Gallimard, 1946.
Translated into English by Douglas Cooper and published by Curt Valentin, New York, 1947.

98a KAHNWEILER, GALERIE, COLLECTION. Catalogue des tableaux . . . [ventes] . . . Hotel Drouot. 4v il Paris, 1921-23.
Sales catalogs listing 183 works by Braque. For prices obtained at sales 1-2, see Esprit Nouveau 2:1565-6, 1825-9 1921.

99 KALLAÏ, ERNÖ. Georges Braque. il Magyar Müvészet (Budapest) 14:289-301 O 1938.
KOBER, JACQUES. See 173.

†100 LALOY, L. [Georges Braque] Comoedia Ja 23 1924.

*101 LEYHAUSEN, KARL. Zu einem Stilleben von Georges Braque. il Kunstblatt 14:102-3 1930.
Analysis of Still Life (1927) by Braque.

102 LHOTE, ANDRÉ. Exposition Braque (Galerie Léonce Rosenberg) Nouvelle Revue Française 6no69:153-7 Je 1 1919.
Reprinted in bibl. 76.

103 —— Le symbolisme plastique de Georges Braque. Nouvelle Revue Française 25e année 48:795-7 My 1937.
Occasioned by exhibition, Galerie Rosenberg, Paris.
* Reprinted in the author's Peinture d'abord. pl59-60 Paris, Denoël, 1942 and in his Ecrits sur la peinture. p278-81 Paris, Editions Lumière, 1946.

*104 —— A propos de Georges Braque. In the author's Peinture d'abord. p157-8 Paris, Denoël, 1942.
* Text dated 1937. Reprinted in the author's Ecrits sur la peinture. p272-6 Paris, Editions Lumière, 1946.
—— See also 172.
McBRIDE, HENRY. See 48, 155, 181.

105 MAKOVSKI, SERGEI. Khudozhestvinnye itogi. Apollon no10:24-34 1910.
Russian text. Discusses French and Russian painting of the 20th century, including Braque and Matisse.

*106 MARTINIE, H. Pariser kunstsommer 1924: Ausstellungen . . . Braque. Der Cicerone 16:751-6 Ag 1924.
Review of exhibition, Galerie Rosenberg, Paris.

*107 MILLER COMPANY, MERIDEN, CONN. Painting toward architecture. p60-1 col il New York, Duell, Sloan and Pearce, 1948.
Brief text accompanying color reproduction of Black Rose, stressing architectural implications of Braque's style.
MORRIS, GEORGE L. K. See 70.

*108 OLIVIER, FERNANDE. Picasso et ses amis. passim Paris, Stock, 1933.
An extract appears in translation in London Studio 7 (Studio 107):199-203 Ap 1934.

*109 PAALEN, WOLFGANG. On the meaning of cubism today. il Dyn (Mexico) 1 no6:4-8 N 1944.
Analysis of Braque painting dated 1912, comparing cubistic technique with musical composition, p5-6.

110 PAULHAN, JEAN. Braque, le patron. 67p 19 col il Paris, Mourlot, 1945.
225 copies printed; contains original color lithograph signed by the artist. Includes "Réflexions par Georges Braque." Some of these statements are reprinted in

* Open Oog (Amsterdam) no1:15-16 S 1946. Text by Paulhan published in Poésie 43; also, translated into

* English in Horizon 11no65:329-39 My 1945. Text with three additional chapters including interview and statements by Braque published by Editions des

* Trois collines, Genève-Paris, 1946, 59p plus 57 plates (1 col). This version published by same publisher in de luxe edition of 90 copies with 2 original lithographs by Braque (1 col), Genève-Paris, 1947.

*111 PÉRET, BENJAMIN. Handle with care [inspired by painting by Braque] In Samuel M. Kootz. Women. p9-11 il New York, S.M. Kootz Editions, 1948.

PHILLIPS, DUNCAN. See 181.

*112 PODESTÀ, ATTILIO. Braque. il por Emporium 108no 613-14:41-4 Jy-Ag 1948.
Occasioned by exhibition at Biennale, Venice, 1948.

*113 PONGE, FRANCIS. Braque, le réconciliateur. 12p il plus 15 col plates Genève, A.Skira, 1946. (Les Trésors de la peinture française)

* Text reprinted in Labyrinthe (Geneva) 2no22-3:6-7 D 1946.

*114 RAYNAL, MAURICE. Georges Braque. 21p il Rome, Editions de "Valori Plastici," 1924.

* Excerpts published in Italian in Valori Plastici (Rome) 2no7-8:83-4;no9-12:107-8 1920 and in French

* in Le Néoclassicisme dans l'art contemporain. p25-6 Rome, Editions de "Valori Plastici," 1923.

*115 —— Anthologie de la peinture en France. p85-92 il Paris, Editions Montaigne, 1927.
Includes statements by Braque, reprinted from bibl.1.

* Published in English in the author's Modern French painters. p50-5 il New York, Brentano's, 1928.

*116 —— Peintres du XXe siècle. p22 col il Genève, A. Skira, 1947. (Trésors de la peinture française)
—— See also 171.

*117 [RÉPRODUCTIONS DE L'OEUVRE DE BRAQUE] il Cahiers d'Art 22:9-36 1947.

*118 ROSENBERG, PAUL. French artists and the war. il (some col) Art in Australia (Sydney) ser4,no4:19-29 D-F 1941-2.
Braque, p26.

*119 ROSENTHAL, GERTRUDE. The art of Georges Braque. il Baltimore Museum of Art News p1-4 Ap 1948.
Includes analysis of Braque's Le Journal.

*120 RUTTER, FRANK. Evolution in modern art. p80,93-6 il London, Harrap, 1926.

RYDBECK-ZUHR, INGRID. See 15.

†121 SALMON, ANDRÉ. L'art vivant. p121 Paris, Crès, 1920.
Reprinted in bibl. 76.

*122 SKIRA, ALBERT, ed. Anthologie du livre illustré par les peintres et sculpteurs de l'école de Paris. p 12 il Genève, Skira, 1946.

†123 SOFFICI, A. Picasso et Braque. La Voce (Florence) Ag 24 1911.
Reprinted in bibl. 76.

†124 SOIRÉES DE PARIS. [Issue devoted to Georges Braque] il Ap 15 1914.

SWEENEY, JAMES JOHNSON. See 155, 181.

*125 TÉRIADE, E. Les dessins de Georges Braque. il Cahiers d'Art 2:141-5 1927.

*126 —— L'épanouissement de l'oeuvre de Braque. il Cahiers d'Art 3no10:409-17 1928.
—— See also 16.

*127 TORRES-GARCÍA, JOAQUIN. Georges Braque. In the author's Universalismo constructivo. p510-12 Buenos Aires, Editorial Poseidon, 1944.

*128 UHDE, WILHELM. Picasso et la tradition française: notes sur la peinture actuelle. p38-41 il Paris, Editions des Quatre chemins, 1928.

* Translated into English in the author's Picasso and the French tradition. p37-41 il Paris, Editions des Quatre chemins, New York, E. Weyhe, 1929.

128a UHDE, WILHELM, COLLECTION. Liste complète des prix atteints aux vente Uhde. Esprit Nouveau 2:1563 1921.
Lists 17 works by Braque.

†129 VAUXCELLES, L. [Georges Braque] Télégramme Ja 5 1909.

†130 —— [Georges Braque] Gil Blas Mr 10 1908, N 14 1908, Mr 25 1909.

*131 VENTURI, LIONELLO. Painting and painters. p210-14 il New York, Scribner's, 1945.
Includes analysis of Platter of Fruit, 1925.

*132 VERONESI, GIULIO. Braque, Picasso, Calder. il Emporium (Milan) 106no635-6:121-3 N-D 1947.
Occasioned by exhibition at Galerie Maeght, Paris.

*133 WALLARD, DANIEL. Braque en 1943. In Gaston Diehl, ed. Les problèmes de la peinture. p93-8 il Paris, Editions Confluences, 1945.

*134 WARNOD, ANDRÉ. Ceux de la butte. p148-9 Paris, René Julliard, 1947.
Brief personal reminiscence.
—— See also 17-18.

*135 WESTHEIM, PAUL. Kunst in Frankreich. il Kunstblatt 6:8-25 1922.
Braque named as leader of cubism, his style very briefly discussed and compared with that of Gris, p10-13.
—— See also 1.

*136 "THE YELLOW CLOTH" GLITTERS. Art Digest 14:5 D 1 1939.
Note indicating prizes won by picture and selling price to current owner.

*137 ZAHAR, MARCEL. Orientation de Georges Braque. In Panorama des arts, 1947. p148-9 il por Paris, Aimery Somogy, 1948.
Occasioned by exhibition at Galerie Maeght, Paris.

*138 ZERVOS, CHRISTIAN. Georges Braque et la peinture française. il Cahiers d'Art 2no1:5-16 1927.
Comparison of Braque and Picasso. 9 illustrations of Braque's paintings, 1925-6, p7,9-16.

139 —— Georges Braque. il Kunst und Künstler 27:386-9 Jy 1929.
Includes biographical information.

*140 ——— Observations sur les peintures récentes de Braque. il Cahiers d'Art 5:5-10 1930.

*141 ——— Le classicisme de Braque. il Cahiers d'Art 6:35-40 1931.

*142 ——— Georges Braque et le développement du cubisme. il por Cahiers d'Art 7no1-2:13-27 1932.
Discussion of Braque's paintings and drawings, 1931; biographical note, p23; also extract from preface to catalog of first Braque exhibition, Kahnweiler gallery, 1908.

*143 ——— Histoire de l'art contemporain. p127,138, 223-34,273-86 il Paris, Editions "Cahiers d'Art," 1938.

*144 ——— Braque et la Grèce primitive. il Cahiers d'Art 15no1-2:3-13 1940.

*145 ——— Georges Braque, Galerie Maeght. il Cahiers d'Art 22:320 1947.

*146 ZOUBALOFF, JACQUES, COLLECTION. Catalogue des tableaux modernes . . . collection Jacques Zoubaloff dont la vente aux enchères . . . aura lieu . . . Hotel Drouot. p5,7,23-4 il Paris, 1935.
Includes 16 works by Braque.

EXHIBITION CATALOGS

Amsterdam
*147 STEDELIJK MUSEUM. Georges Braque: Catalogus van de Tentoonstelling . . . 20 October-12 November 1945. 6p il.
Lists 26 works.

Avignon
*148 PALAIS DES PAPES. Exposition de peintures et sculptures contemporaines . . . du 27 juin au 30 septembre 1947. 92p il.
Lists 13 works by Braque, p10. Stylistic comments, p35-6. Reprint of statement by Braque on back cover.

Baltimore
149 MUSEUM OF ART. Georges Braque, November 22-December 27 1942. 1p.
Typewritten sheet listing 16 works.

Basel
*150 KUNSTHALLE. Georges Braque. 9. April-14. Mai 1933. 23p il.
Lists 183 works. Preface by Carl Einstein. Reviewed in Werk 20 hft5:xxx S 1930. See also bibl. 76.

151 ——— Juan Gris, Georges Braque, Pablo Picasso, 26. Febr.-24. März 1948. 24p.
Lists 40 works by Braque.

Berlin
152 FLECHTHEIM, ALFRED, GALERIE. Matisse, Braque, Picasso, 21. September bis mitte Oktober 1930. 24p il.
Lists 24 works by Braque, p10-14. Reviewed in Apollo 12:372-3 N 1930.

Berne
153 KUNSTHALLE. Georges Braque, Juan Gris, Pablo Picasso. 2. bis 29. April 1948. 14p.
Lists 37 works by Braque, p9-10. Reviewed in Werk 35hft4:sup37 Ap 1948.

Brussels
154 PALAIS DES BEAUX ARTS. Georges Braque, novembre-décembre 1936. 16p il.
Lists 81 works. Reviewed in Amour de l'Art 18:64 F 1937.

——— Georges Braque. Du 24 novembre au 13 décembre 1945. 7p.
Lists 27 works.

Chicago
*155 ARTS CLUB OF CHICAGO. Georges Braque: retrospective exhibition . . . November seventh to twenty-seventh 1939. 11p il.
Preface by Henry McBride, foreword by James Johnson Sweeney, and facsimile of letter to Mrs. Goodspeed. Lists 68 works.

London
*156 REID, ALEX. & LEFEVRE, LTD. Paintings by Georges Braque, July 1934. 10p il.
Lists 41 works. Reviewed in Apollo 20no116:104 Ag 1934.

156a ROSENBERG & HELFT, LTD. Exhibition of masterpieces by Braque, Matisse, Picasso, October 5th-mid November 1936. 11p il.
Lists 14 works by Braque. Reviewed in Apollo 24no143:301 N 1936.

*157 ——— Exhibition: recent works of Braque. [July] 1938. 3p.
Lists 22 works.

*158 ——— Exhibition: Braque, recent works . . . 6th June to 8th July 1939. 3p il.
Lists 24 works. Reviewed in Studio 117:82-3 F 1939.

*159 TATE GALLERY. Braque and Rouault. 1946. 11p.
Lists 28 works by Braque. Introduction by Germain
* Bazin. Reviewed in Connoisseur 117:123-4 Je 1946;
* in Studio 132:21 Jy 1946 and in Art News 42:43 Je 1946.

New York
*160 BUCHHOLZ GALLERY. Some selected paintings by G. Braque. October 14th to 29th 1938. 3p il.
* Lists 16 works. Reviewed in Art News 37:14 O 22 1938.
DURAND-RUEL. For review of exhibition (1934) and catalog see 58.

*161 MUSEUM OF FRENCH ART. Picasso, Braque, Léger: loan exhibition, February 1931. 4p.
Lists 5 works by Braque. Foreword by Maud Dale. Reviewed in Apollo 13:238 Ap 1931.

*162 MUSEUM OF MODERN ART. Cubism and abstract art [ed. by Alfred H. Barr, Jr.] 1936. passim p205 il.
Lists 9 works by Braque. Includes biographical and bibliographical notes.

*163 ROSENBERG, PAUL. Exhibition of paintings by Braque. April 7th-25th 1942. 3p.
* Lists 13 works. Reviewed in Art Digest 16:10 Ap 15
* 1942; Art News 41:33 My 1 1942.

*164 ——— Paintings by Braque and Picasso . . . April 6th-May 1st 1943. 3p.

* Lists 6 works. Reviewed in Art Digest 17:14 Ap 15 1943.

*165 ——— Exhibition of paintings: Braque, Matisse, Picasso . . . November 6th to December 2nd 1944. 3p. Lists 4 works by Braque.

*166 ——— Paintings by Braque. April 29th to May 18th 1946. 3p.

* Lists 11 works. Reviewed in Art News 45:58 My
* 1946 and in Art Digest 20:12 My 1 1946.

*167 ——— Paintings by Braque. January 5th to 24th 1948. 3p.
Lists 15 works. Reviewed in Art News 46:40 Ja 1948; in Art Digest 22:11 Ja 15 1948.

*168 VALENTINE GALLERY. Exhibition of recent paintings by Georges Braque. November 26-December 15, 1934. 2p.
Lists 16 works. Reviewed in Art News 33:6 D 8 1934.

169 ——— An exhibition of paintings by Georges Braque. January 13th to February 8th 1941. 2p.
Lists 27 works. Reviewed in Art News 39:15 Ja 25 1941.

Paris
*170 "BEAUX ARTS" & "GAZETTE DES BEAUX ARTS." Les créateurs du cubisme, mars-avril 1935. 33p il. (Les Etapes de l'art contemporain. 5)
Lists 25 works by Braque. Preface by Maurice Raynal and text by Raymond Cogniat.

*171 GALERIE DE FRANCE. Le cubisme, 1911-1918. Du 25 mai au 30 juin 1945. 59p il.
Lists 9 works by Braque, p31, biographical note, p21. Introductory text by Bernard Dorival, note on Braque's *La Guitare* (1913) by André Lhote.
KAHNWEILER, GALERIE. For preface to exhibition catalog by Apollinaire, see bibl. 142.

*172 MAEGHT, GALERIE. G. Braque. *In* Derrière le Miroir, Je 1947, 8p il (some col).
Lists 58 works by Braque. Includes text by René Char, reprinted in Cahiers d'Art 22:334 1947, Jacques Kober, and quotations and page extracted from notebooks of Braque. Reviewed in bibl. 49, 132, 137, 145.

*173 PETIT PALAIS. Les maîtres de l'art indépendant, 1895-1937. Juin-octobre 1937. 120p il.
Lists 29 works by Braque, p96-7. Reviewed in Beaux Arts no235:8 Je 2 1937.
PIERRE, GALERIE. For review of exhibition (1938) see bibl. 33.
ROSENBERG, LÉONCE. For review of exhibitions (1919) see bibl. 30, 102; (1924) see bibl. 106; (1926) see bibl. 86.

*174 ROSENBERG, PAUL. Exposition d'oeuvres récentes de Georges Braque du . . . 8 janvier au . . . 31 janvier 1936. 8p il.
Lists 20 works. Reviewed in Amour de l'Art 17no4: 151-2 Ap 1936.

*175 ——— Exposition d'oeuvres récentes de Georges Braque du . . . 3 avril au . . . 30 avril 1937. 5p il.
Lists 18 works. Reviewed in bibl. 77, 103.

*176 ——— Exposition Braque du . . . 16 novembre au . . . 10 décembre 1938. 3p.
Lists 22 works. Reviewed in Studio 117:82 F 1939 and in Renaissance 21:44 Ja 1939.

177 ——— Exposition Braque (oeuvres récentes) du 4 au 29 avril 1939. 3p il.
Lists 27 works. Reviewed in Studio 118:35 Jy 1939, in Emporium 90:40 Jy 1939, and in bibl. 27.

Stockholm
*178 LILJEVALCHS KONSTHALL. Henri Matisse, Picasso, Braque, Laurens. 1938. 32p il.
Lists 39 works by Braque, p26. Text by Walther Halvorsen, p21-5. Extract translated into French in Cahiers d'Art 12:218-21 1937. Exhibition prepared in Sweden by Föreningen för nutida konst. Also shown in Oslo, Copenhagen, Göteborg.

Venice
179 BIENNALE DI VENEZIA, XXIV. Catalogo. 4a ed. definitiva. p266-8,339 Venezia, Serenissima, 1948.
Lists 20 works by Braque, 2 in Peggy Guggenheim collection. Note by Raymond Cogniat. Reviewed in
† bibl. 112.

Washington, D.C.
180 PHILLIPS MEMORIAL GALLERY. Georges Braque retrospective exhibition, December 6 1939 to January 6 1940. 8p il.
Lists 55 works. Introduction by Duncan Phillips, biographical note by Henry McBride (as in bibl. 155) and an appreciation by James Johnson Sweeney (as in bibl. 155). Reviewed in Art News 38:10 Ja 6 1940.

Zurich
181 KUNSTHAUS. Georges Braque, Wassily Kandinsky, Pable Picasso. 21. September bis 20. Oktober 1946. 22p.
Lists 26 works by Braque, p3-5. Reviewed in bibl. 28, 78.

183 ——— Gustav Gamper . . . Augusto Giacometti . . Aus schweizerischen Privatsammlungen: Braque, Gris, Picasso. 23p.
Lists 25 works by Braque, p12.

This book has been printed in February, 1949, for the Trustees of the Museum of Modern Art, New York by the Plantin Press, New York. The color plates have been printed by Davis, Delaney, Inc., New York. Cover and typography by Edward L. Mills

PB-36164
551-09